BIOGRAPHIES FOR 8TH GRADE HISTORY

TWENTY REMARKABLE MEN AND WOMEN

Biographies for 8th Grade History

Twenty Remarkable Men and Women

by

Susan Cook

Waldorf
PUBLICATIONS
RESEARCH INSTITUTE FOR WALDORF EDUCATION

DEDICATION

To all children, spouses and partners of class teachers,
starting with my own—
Peter, Jason, James and Lauren
—for your endless patience and support.

Published with the support of the
Waldorf Educational Foundation

Waldorf Publications at the
Research Institute of Waldorf Education
351 Fairview Avenue Unit 625
Hudson, NY 12534

Title: *Biographies for 8th Grade History:*
  Twenty Remarkable Men and Women
Author: Susan Cook
Editor: David Mitchell

Second edition November 2020
ISBN: 978-1-943582-50-1

TABLE OF CONTENTS

INTRODUCTION

This book of biographies is the result of a perceived need I experienced as an eighth grade teacher for an anthology of key historical figures tailored to the developmental interests of my students and charged with the dynamic themes of global influence and revolution. But as any eighth grade teacher will tell you amid the tumult of class play, main lesson, field trips and graduation, "The need for a book is here, but when is there time to write it?" During four terms as an eighth grade teacher, my biography anthology simmered—perhaps developed a richer complexity of flavors. A sabbatical last year let me pull my parcels from the pantry and transform them into a book I hope will stimulate your own individual instruction.

Eighth grade history in the Waldorf curriculum is simply overwhelming in scope, and careful choices must be made that both characterize the stages of history in the last three-and-a-half centuries and pay tribute to movers and shakers in your region. Most names in this collection are familiar, but I have omitted many of the usual biographical conventions. My intention is to focus on two key points: 1) the inclusion of international perspective and 2) a demonstration of the spirit of revolution in a variety of fields. The collection is distinctly American—I teach in San Francisco—but there are important representatives from other countries. Because of my association with the Rudolf Steiner School Mbagathi near Nairobi, I have included two Kenyan biographies as well.

For my collection I have also chosen to focus on the younger years of each person, which has been a proven way to engage the sympathy and interest of my students. Physical descriptions and unique character traits are also key components to a lively presentation. By including a vivid episode from childhood, for example, the story is bound to make a lasting impression on the class.

How one tells the tale is as essential as what goes into it—a caution all Waldorf teachers know. Telling the story of the "Golden Goose" to kindergartners is not the same as relating a biography of Gandhi to eighth graders, but there is a long, evolving line between the two. When kindergartners take in a story, their wiggling slowly ceases, eyes glisten wide and mouths open softly. The young children drink in the tale with their entire being. Young teens, by contrast, engage in multiple distracting actions as they appear to defiantly not-listen. But it is remarkable what they toss back to the teacher when asked to recall the details the following day.

In Waldorf schools the oral tradition remains a powerful, guaranteed method of imparting important pedagogical substance that touches the sympathies and antipathies of the students. Through this engagement with the emotions, a response is struck in each student's feeling life that rises into the cognitive sphere, becoming available content for future ideas and concepts. A practiced teacher knows how to make the most of a story by directing specific details to the student who will benefit most. Clara Barton's struggle with extreme shyness, Marie Curie's insatiable passion for science, Frederick Douglass's mistreatment as a slave—all resonate differently with each child.

Today, in this era of standardized accountability and paper trails, the art of storytelling has disappeared from most teachers' repertoires. And yet the value of imparted wisdom via story remains a profoundly human need in our time. My book is a gift to Waldorf teachers in their efforts to keep the storytelling impulse alive and to place it solidly in the classrooms of the future. I would like to thank San Francisco Waldorf School for a sabbatical that provided me with the time to cull favorite stories from years of joyful teaching and to transform thought to deeds.

JOHN HARRISON
(1693–1776)

Significance: For centuries mariners were unable to establish their longitude at sea, and Harrison solved the problem by designing a clock that would work under seafaring conditions. Before Harrison's clock, mariners had no reliable method of knowing the distances traveled in the east-west direction, leading to fear and sometimes disaster.

Background: Facts of Latitude and Longitude

Latitude is the height of the sun or guide star(s) above the horizon. As long as you know the time of year, you can determine the north/south location by the angle of the sun or guide star (Polaris in the northern hemisphere). For a northern hemisphere example, if your ship drifts southward during the winter months, the angle of the sun above the horizon will diminish quickly; the change in the length of daylight is a tip-off. We think of latitude as the arbitrary lines drawn on a globe or map that are horizontal to the equator. Measured in degrees of a sphere, there are 90 degrees from the equator to either pole, 180 degrees from North Pole to South Pole, and 360 degrees circumscribing the globe through the poles. Columbus "sailed the parallel," following the well traveled routes of ancient mariners and cagey pirates across the mid-Atlantic.

Longitude is a very different measurement from latitude. It measures the east-west location (from an arbitrarily established line of 0 degrees at Greenwich, London, England), rather than the north-south distance from the equator. Consider the distance around the equator in terms of 360 degrees of a circle, and divide that distance into 24 equal "hours," which means each hour is 15 degrees (360/24 = 15). At the equator each 15 degrees equals a distance of roughly 1000 miles, but at either pole the distance is exactly zero! Lay the pieces of the globe out flat and it is shaped much like wedges of a pie. Longitude lines are not parallel like latitudes; they converge at the poles.

To determine longitude, three steps must be followed: 1) a clock must be set to the time at the home port, 2) a clock must be set to the time at the current location at sea, using the sun or guide star and 3) the difference in time multiplied by 15 degrees longitude is the distance between the two points, assuming the latitude does not change.

The problem is determining the precise hour at two places at once! The 15th, 16th, 17th and 18th centuries represent 400 years of trying. It was like looking for the

Fountain of Youth, seemingly as illusive but nearly as desirable. There would be untold riches for the country that held the secret because they could control the seas. The old method was called dead reckoning, and it unfortunately often meant a dead man, or men, from scurvy or other perils. The method was very inexact: throw a log overboard, estimate the speed and multiply by the time measured with an hourglass—all of this in a stormy sea.

In 1610 Galileo had thought to solve the problem through astronomy, and he designed a navigational helmet using the moons of Jupiter. Then in 1637 he had a further idea with a pendulum clock, but he never finished.

There was one especially crazy idea that gained favor for a short time: A fleet of ships would be anchored on a grid at 600-mile intervals throughout the entire Atlantic Ocean. At that time it was assumed that the deepest part of the North Atlantic was 300 fathoms, when in fact the floor of the ocean is 2000 fathoms or more. The idea of anchors reaching so deep was impossible, plus who would volunteer to live on the ships? And how many ships would it take?

The Longitude Act of 1714 was passed in England, offering 20,000£ to anyone who could devise a method to find a ship's longitude anywhere on earth to an accuracy of ½ degree, or equal to 30 minutes of longitude. The public was well aware of the contest, and every scientifically inclined mind was tuned to the situation. ◆

John Harrison was born on March 24, 1693, in Yorkshire, the eldest of five children. Most of the family members were named Henry, John, or Elizabeth. The name Elizabeth, for example, belonged to his mother, sister, both wives, his daughter and his two daughters-in-law. Very little is known about his childhood, but it is safe to assume that he did his fair share of farm chores and attended school sporadically, if at all. He was physically of average size with a long thin face and arching eyebrows poised above watchful eyes that quietly observed nature and the events around him.

In spite of his father's modest means, Harrison was exposed to book learning and local cultural opportunities. He learned music and played the violin. He craved books, especially scientific ones, and he once borrowed a book on mechanics and copied it all. For Shakespeare, however, he had no use. His first employment was as a carpenter on the estate where he was born.

Harrison completed his first pendulum clock by age 20. It was a carpenter's clock, constructed almost exclusively out of wood. Clocks and watches at the time were rare, and thus exceedingly expensive. The Harrison family certainly didn't own one, so it is a question where he would have studied one as a model.

Harrison married twice; his first wife died. There were two children from his second marriage, William and Elizabeth, and in time William became his father's assistant.

Everyone knew about the longitude problem, so it is no surprise that Harrison was interested. Most pendulums of the day slowed down in warmer weather and sped up with colder temperatures. He fixed that problem by combining strips of two different metals – brass and steel – in one pendulum, resulting in a clock that was accurate to a second at the end of the month. As he contemplated the image of pendulums on the rolling seas, he pictured a springing set of seesaws.

Spurred by the competition and prize money, work on the clock that would operate accurately at sea (called a marine chronometer) occupied most of his life, and although he was successful, he was never properly satisfied and continually tried for improvements. The first completed sea clock was called the H-1, and it took him five years to construct. It was a huge time machine looking like a model ship, weighing 75 pounds. It is still working today! But he wasn't satisfied. He asked the Royal Commission for their blessing to try again, and he produced H-2 which weighed 86 pounds and still did not meet his expectations.

Harrison's design was based on the concept that a clock set to the exact time at Greenwich, England (0 degrees longitude, also called Prime Meridian), would be carried on a ship and read at exactly 12 noon, local time, determined by the sun directly overhead. The time difference would be multiplied by 15 degrees, because the earth revolves 360 degrees in 24 hours, which is 15 degrees per hour. The result would be the ship's longitude.

He spent nearly 20 years on H-3. Meanwhile his own clock was ticking. He completed his fourth chronometer, H-4, in 1759, and it was carried across the Atlantic Ocean from England to Jamaica and back during a five-month sea trial in 1761 and 1762. Harrison's clock was found to have an error of only 1¼ minutes, which surpassed the requirements for the prize. The Royal Commission was loath to award such a prestigious award to someone of such low social standing, and they paid him only small increments until King George III heard about it and intervened on his behalf.

Harrison died on March 24, 1776, exactly 83 years old.

ELI WHITNEY
(1765–1825)

Significance: Cotton represented the most important industry in the United States in the early 19th century, due largely to Eli Whitney's invention of the cotton gin. He is also credited with developing the idea of interchangeable parts, crucial to the growth of factories in the Industrial Revolution.

Slavery in the United States almost came to a quiet end at the close of the 18th century. The Southern economy was slipping, and the focus of the young and energetic section of the population was westward to the land of opportunity. The farmland in the South had been overworked, especially by intensive tobacco farming, and fewer slaves were needed to work the land. In 1808 a law was passed banning the importation of any more slaves, and one would have thought that the days of slavery were numbered.

Eli Whitney was a Northerner, and he never intended to affect the existence of slavery one way or the other. Born on December 8, 1765, he grew up as the oldest son of a Massachusetts farming family. He had wavy dark brown hair, sad eyes with circles beneath, and a small mouth.

Like most farms, there was a workshop for storing and repairing farm equipment, and Eli spent many hours there tinkering with machines. At an early age he could take a watch apart and reassemble it, and when he was twelve, he made himself a violin. During the Revolutionary War Eli was too young to serve as a soldier, but he contributed to the cause by supplying much-needed nails to the army. After the war ended, he continued his business until he entered college at age 23. When the demand for nails decreased, his eye for business fell upon ladies' hatpins and men's walking sticks which were popular at the time. He turned the walking sticks on his father's lathe and added the metal piece from the forge.

Desperate for a job after he finished his schooling at Yale College, he accepted a position as a teacher in South Carolina. During the journey he met by chance Katherine Greene, the widow of Revolutionary War hero, General Nathaniel Greene, and was invited to be a guest at her plantation near Savannah, Georgia. To a young man accustomed to the harsh New England winters, the South must have been a tremendous shock with its balmy temperatures, lush and exotic plant life and gentile lifestyle. Being a poor conversationalist and uneasy in the plantation social life, he spent time in the workshop making repairs and tinkering with mechanical things. He probably thought he should do something to make himself useful while he enjoyed Mrs. Greene's Southern hospitality.

One evening as he was sitting in the background, a group of planters were complaining about the difficulty of making any money growing cotton. The type of cotton that grew in the area was short-staple, and it was full of obstinate seeds that had to be laboriously removed by hand. It took a whole day for one slave to clean just one pound of cotton. They spoke bitterly about the long-staple cotton that the Northerners were importing cheaply to spin cotton thread using the new spinning jennies. A spinning jenny was an advanced type of spinning wheel that filled dozens of spindles simultaneously using the power of a single water wheel. The Southern farmers could not hope to compete with the imported cotton, and their economic prospects were declining.

The problem of cleaning cotton stuck in Whitney's mind, and he began a series of experiments in the plantation workshop. He tried all kinds of boxes, cylinders, blades and raking devices. Much later Whitney wrote to a friend about how his idea arose. While thinking about the cotton problem, he was absentmindedly watching a cat reach his claws through a wire mesh fence into a chicken coop. The cat put one claw through the fence and held completely still, waiting for an unsuspecting chicken to walk by. When a chicken came close, the cat snatched, missed the chicken but came up with a pawful of feathers. He applied the same idea to cotton and within a week invented the cotton gin. Without meaning to do anything more than solve a vexing problem, Whitney made a small invention that produced the Cotton Kingdom in the South.

Whitney lived during the era of the Industrial Revolution when inventors were designing simple machines to do work faster and more efficiently than people. The way in which people made their living was changing rapidly. Many left their farms and flocked to the cities in search of jobs in the new factories that were springing up. During this time the belief was strong that machines had unlimited potential for improving society. Whitney realized that no matter what machine was being manufactured, it was extremely advantageous to reproduce each part with exact precision so that parts were interchangeable. Before the Industrial Revolution, for example, each part of a musket was handmade by a gunsmith and there was no uniform pattern.

Although Whitney's cotton gin was highly successful and led to economic renewal in the South, the invention did not bring him the wealth he had hoped for. The patent he held did not prevent others from copying his cotton gin, and the legal and business hassles left him physically weakened and dispirited. Nevertheless, his interests remained in inventions, and he never gave teaching a thought again.

In the early 1800s, he moved on to another project, producing muskets for the United States army, and this time he was wise to avoid previous mistakes. He signed a contract to deliver ten thousand muskets in two years' time, and no one thought he could possibly do it. His system was to invent separate machines to turn out each part, thus replacing the traditional handwork of skilled craftsmen. Other inventors were working on the same idea, and there was an atmosphere of urgency and competitiveness in the air. In the end Whitney needed more time, but his technique was successful and the government granted him an extension on his deadline and more money. Whitney laid the groundwork for today's assembly lines, which produce thousands of items to exact specifications with speed and at low cost.

Eli Whitney was a dedicated man who devoted all of his waking hours to his business and inventions. He was given honors by universities and scientific groups, and President Thomas Jefferson, himself an inventor, was a supporter of his ideas. With all of his projects Whitney had no time for a family, and his only friends were work-related. He literally lived in his workshop.

Then at the age of 52, he married 31-year-old Henrietta Edwards, the daughter of a business friend. By this time he had grown a bit portly and sported carefully clipped sideburns which were very fashionable. During their eight years of marriage they had four children, and the death of one in infancy was a terrible blow to him.

Whitney was plagued with continuing health issues that were probably exacerbated by his work pressures. He died in 1825, at the age of 60, a man well recognized for his contributions to his country. His cotton gin had brought new life to the economy of the South—and, tragically, a prolonged demand for slaves—and his muskets established the machine tool industry in the Northern states.

SEQUOYAH
(CIRCA 1770–1843)

Significance: The background for Sequoyah's biography is the forced removal of the Cherokee and other Native American nations between 1825 and 1850 to the "Indian Territory" west of the Mississippi. Sequoyah is famous for creating a writing system for the Cherokee language.

Sequoyah grew up in the Great Smoky Mountains which are often cloaked in a bluish mist that stretches far into the distance. Part of current-day Tennessee, the hills are rugged and thick with towering poplars, white oaks and huge, drooping willows. According to Cherokee elders, the world began when the Great Buzzard flapped his strong wings against the soft mud of the newly formed earth. Each time his wing stroked downward and touched the earth, a valley was created, and each time his wing stroked upward, a mountain was formed. The Cherokees might have lived on a flat landscape if it hadn't been for the Great Buzzard causing all the mountains to come into existence.

As a boy, Sequoyah walked in the woods and forests, learned to recognize the bird songs and spot their hidden nests, and discovered how to set traps and nets for wild turkeys and to fish in the streams. His mother Wuh-teh showed him how to test the soil between his fingers and to smell it to see if it was warm enough for planting corn. Sequoyah's father was a white man, probably a trader, who left the Cherokee community before his son was old enough to remember him. His uncles, especially the one who was the town chief, were important guides in his life.

As an only child he spent many hours alone, and during this solitude time he entertained himself by sketching with a bit of charcoal on pieces of bark. His mother encouraged his drawing, and others began to take notice of his unusual abilities, commenting that he showed promise as someone who would serve his tribe.

The Cherokees relied on oral tradition to hand down their stories and beliefs, much as all other Native American tribes. Their storytellers memorized and repeated all the history of the tribe and could recite from memory for hours. There were also tales for entertainment, and many included lessons about the important values of the Cherokee, such as honesty over treachery and good over evil.

Sequoyah also loved the ball game, similar to lacrosse, which the Cherokee played, even though he was destined to sit on the sidelines. A birth defect or childhood accident had caused one of his legs to be weaker than the other, and he walked with a limp. His name "Sequoyah" is said to be derived from a Cherokee word meaning "pig's foot." Others suggest his name means "sand hill crane," after the bird that stands on one foot. In spite of his disability, he rode a horse with great skill and was an accomplished hunter. His prominent nose, deep-set dark eyes and gentle mouth added to his overall distinguished appearance.

As Sequoyah was growing into adulthood, a troubling time was settling over his tribe. White settlers were setting up homes in the Cherokee homelands and intruding on the ancient ways of his people. Armed conflict broke out in isolated incidents; Cherokee warriors attacked and settlers fought back, sometimes by burning entire villages. Promises to respect Cherokee boundaries were repeatedly violated, and displacement became a familiar occurrence.

As a young man, Sequoyah established a successful trading business with his mother. He also became well known for his artistic talents. He taught himself silversmithing, and his unusually fine silver items were sought after by his tribesmen who appreciated such high quality jewelry and ornaments. In an effort to put his personal mark on each item he created, he learned how to spell his name and stamp it on each piece of silver work he made. His business grew and he expanded into blacksmithing, teaching himself the craft and building his own forge, bellows and tools.

Keeping track of the money owed by his various customers began to tax Sequoyah's memory capacity, so he devised an accounting method with a picture of each person with tally marks for money owed.

One day Sequoyah was in the middle of a conversation with a group of men, and they were discussing whether white people had invented talking leaves (messages written on paper) themselves or whether they had received that ability as a gift from the Creator Spirit. Most Cherokees accepted the second explanation, and there was even an often-told story in support that said the first man on earth, an Indian, had received a written book as a gift from the Creator. When he wasn't looking, a white man crept up and stole the book, leaving a bow and arrow in its place.

Sequoyah scoffed at such a story. From his experience of putting his stamped name on his handcrafts, he was beginning to realize that a message with written marks could be created between a sender and a receiver, just as long as both parties agreed ahead of time what the marks stood for. The others belittled his idea, but he was certain that he could make marks that could be understood by someone else. His mind was fixed on the idea of capturing Cherokee speech with marks on paper.

Sequoyah became possessed with his desire to preserve the Cherokee language in written form. More and more of the young people were learning English, and he feared that his language would disappear. The beautiful Cherokee language represented the ancestors back through time, the heart of the people, the sighing of the forest, the rushing of the mountain stream. It was the most precious thing to Sequoyah, and he wanted to preserve it for all time by committing it to paper in written form. He wanted to make talking leaves that spoke the Cherokee language and served the purposes of his tribe.

For a long time as he worked, he devoted himself to studying the sounds around him. He listened closely to the chirping of different birds, the hooting of owls and the chatter of squirrels. He began to amass a huge inventory of pictures to accompany spoken ideas. "A horse with a black mane" was one picture; "a horse with a black mane and white marking" was another picture, and so on—eventually resulting in thousands of variations. Sequoyah became obsessed with his project, doing nothing else to the point that his wife Sally and his neighbors thought he was overcome by evil spirits. One day he left his cabin where he worked continually, and his wife and neighbors set it ablaze. All the years of his labor turned to ashes.

Although the fire was a terrible shock to him and everything was lost, afterward Sequoyah was forced to try a new approach, one that proved much more workable in the end. In a moment of inspiration, it came to him that a writing system did not need to depend on a new symbol for every separate meaning. He suddenly realized that his language was put together by a certain limited number of sounds that came in a multitude of combinations. If he could create a symbol to represent each sound, he could unlock the mystery of written Cherokee—any word could be written! According to his ear, there were just over two hundred different possible syllables, and he drew a symbol for each. The letters he fashioned were his own unique, swirling creations. (Later the number was reduced to 85.)

It took some effort to convince his tribesmen that he was actually reading the Cherokee language from pieces of paper. Everyone thought he had just memorized the messages, and they were unimpressed. One day he performed a demonstration with his daughter Ah-yo-kah that converted skeptics. Sequoyah and his daughter stood before a gathering of his people to show how his writing invention worked. He sent Ah-yo-kah some distance away where she could not hear what was said. Then one person was asked to speak a message to Sequoyah which he wrote down on paper. Ah-yo-kah was called back to speak the message by looking at the paper and without looking at her father. Confidently she sounded out the syllables to speak the message. The people were so surprised. They tried the same thing again, and again she spoke the message correctly. Sequoyah had to repeat the test with several young men before his people were truly convinced, but finally his accomplishment was recognized. He had given the Cherokee people their own talking leaves! At last they accepted his gift of literacy.

Sequoyah's alphabet, called a syllabary, was the talk of the Cherokee nation. The people were proud that their language could be used to send messages long distances, and many quickly learned how to use it.

Sequoyah is the only individual in all recorded history known to have devised a complete writing system without first being literate in some language. He not only created the symbols for the sounds, but he had also conceived the idea of a written language with only a vague hint from the talking leaves of white people to go on. Speeches of the chiefs of the past were faithfully recorded for posterity. Records were made of all Council meetings. Soon there was a Cherokee newspaper, the first bilingual one ever, and almost all Cherokees became literate. Unfortunately, not all the news was good for the Cherokee nation.

During the 1820s and 1830s, life in Cherokee territory became more and more dangerous. White people continued to push into their land, causing Indians to raid and kill; whites retaliated with superior numbers and weapons. Many settlers died, but the Cherokee were losing far more through the additional factor of disease. More and more, the U.S. government took the position that all Indians should live west of the Mississippi where there was plenty of land and they could live in peace, or so it was believed at the time.

In 1839 Sequoyah emigrated west, along with thousands of his people, to present-day Oklahoma, which became known as Indian Territory. He was one of the voluntary settlers, but in a few years many thousands more would come, and not by choice. In fact, between 1825 and 1850 nearly all Native Americans —

Choctaw, Creek, Seminole, Chickasaw, Shawnee and even more tribes—were forced to move west during a prolonged period of Indian removal promoted by the very popular president, Andrew Jackson.

The Cherokee stubbornly resisted leaving their homeland, and, empowered with their own writing, they took their land claims in a case argued before the Supreme Court (Worcester v. Georgia). In the court's ruling on the issue of Indian ownership of their own land, Chief Justice John Marshall wrote:

"The Cherokee nation, then, is a distinct community, occupying its own territory...in which the laws of Georgia can have no force, and which the citizens of Georgia have no right to enter, but with the assent of the Cherokees themselves."

The Cherokee both won and lost. They won the case before the Supreme Court, but they lost their cause because President Jackson refused to enforce the law. It is not a proud chapter of American history. In what became known as the "Trail of Tears," the Cherokees—children, parents, the elderly—walked west against their wishes in often harsh weather without proper food or shelter. Always there was overwhelming sadness, for approximately one fourth of them died on the cruel march.

The final chapter of Sequoyah's life took him to Mexico where he was determined to take his gift of written Cherokee to a band of his people who had emigrated there. He died near a town called San Fernando, in what is now Texas, in August 1843.

His accomplishment of developing a writing system for the Cherokee language gave his people an important tool for the future while creating a way to preserve their past treasures. The giant sequoia trees and Sequoia National Park in California are named in his honor.

SIMÓN BOLIVAR
(1783–1830)

Significance: Bolivar was instrumental in ousting the Spanish from their colonial holdings in South America, and he is considered today one of the greatest Hispanic heroes.

Since the beginning of colonial control in the 1500s, Venezuela has had five distinct classes of people, and the mixture has made Venezuelans a difficult people to rule. At the top of the social ladder came the officials from Spain who ran the country when it was a colony. Second were the Creoles, who were Spaniards born in Venezuela; third were the mestizos, or people of mixed European and Indian ancestry; fourth were the mulattoes, or people of mixed Spanish and Negro origin; and fifth were the indigenous people, generally referred to as Indians. From the beginning of colonial rule, Spain kept a harsh rein on the Venezuelans, and all important government positions were filled by Spaniards coming directly from the court in Spain.

Spain controlled virtually all trade with Venezuela, and other foreign governments and their trading companies detested Spain's harsh monopoly. Sooner or later this intolerable situation was bound to boil over into a major struggle between Spain and Venezuela, her major colony in South America. The American Revolution in 1776, in which people had fought against intolerable government control, and the French Revolution in 1789, in which people had risen against unendurable conditions—both of these revolutions served as inspirations for several failed attempts in Venezuela to overthrow the Spaniards. Venezuela was waiting for a true leader to be born who could unite all the classes of the people in a successful revolt.

On July 24, 1783, Simón Bolivar was born into a Creole family that had been in Venezuela more than two hundred years. The name Bolivar means "the field near the mill," suggesting perhaps that the family had long been landowners, even back in Spain. In Venezuela they bought up huge tracts of land; they planted coffee and cocoa and mined for copper. The family owned many homes, huge farms and ranches with large herds of cattle. His father, Colonel Juan Vicente Bolivar, married his mother, Dona Marie de la Concepcion, when he was 47 years old and she was only 15. They had four children, and Simón was the youngest.

Simón was born with everything a young boy could possibly desire, including a handsome appearance. He was tall with dark, flashing eyes, black hair and an air of confidence in his movements that showed to great advantage when, dressed in shiny leather boots and the finest riding outfit, he rode his horse. The family's main house in the city was a huge mansion with gardens, and their country estate lay beside a river filled with fish. They were millionaires many times over. Records show that his two sisters had an income of $50,000 a year, enormous in those days. With such wealth and position in society, it is unimaginable that the Bolivars could ever become revolutionaries. But Simón was orphaned early in life. Dates vary, but his father died when he was between the ages of three and six. A few short years later his mother died suddenly of a fever. However, wealthy relatives surrounded the children, and Simón grew up both spoiled and precocious.

When he first began school, Simón was taught by cowled monks who studiously followed the dictates of Spain and the Catholic Church. The lessons were lifeless, boring repetitions of authorized texts. Then, when Simón was eleven years old, his uncle and guardian hired a private tutor named Simón Rodriguez, and the two Simóns quickly formed a permanent friendship. Rodriguez was a young man bursting with new ideas, and he tossed the young Simón's old-fashioned textbooks into the wastepaper basket. Soon they were studying about the French Revolution and the concepts of democracy, equality and justice. Rodriguez opened his young student's eyes to the bad treatment of Indians and black slaves in Venezuela. Simón's education was excellent and thorough, but it was fortunate that what he was learning did not come to the attention of the authorities. Their disapproval would no doubt have led to the hanging of Rodriguez for treasonous behavior.

Young wealthy Creoles were often sent to Spain to complete their education, and at age sixteen Simón was thrilled to travel to Madrid to live with another uncle. Putting revolutionary ideas aside for the time being, he indulged in a busy social life of parties and banquets with his many new friends of the privileged class.

Once he was playing a game of tennis with Ferdinand, the king's eldest son, and he arrogantly served the ball straight at the prince's head, thus causing him to duck to avoid being hit. There is an unwritten rule that royalty is not treated in an undignified manner, and the conceited young prince was so furious that he immediately challenged Simón to a duel. The queen quickly intervened, which was fortunate for Ferdinand because Simón was a far superior duelist.

At the age of seventeen, Simón met Marie Teresa Rodriguez de Toro, a tall, black-haired beauty, and he fell in love with her. He had to wait two long years until he was nineteen to marry her. The happy couple moved to Venezuela to live at one of the Bolivar estates, and this period was probably the most contented of Simón's life. The political future of Venezuela was not yet a concern. But then, after only eight months of marriage, Marie fell sick with yellow fever and died. Simón was quoted at the time as saying, "I shall never marry again. I shall spend the rest of my life remembering the happy days

Marie and I enjoyed together." And true to his word, he never did marry again.

Bolivar sailed for Europe and the renewed company of his elegant friends. For a while he lived in Paris, gaining a reputation for spending large sums on clothes, parties, gambling and horses. It was an exciting time in Paris because Napoleon, the ruler of France, had decided to crown himself like Caesar. Bolivar had admired Napoleon as a commoner who had the intelligence and audacity to rise to the very top, but he changed his opinion when Napoleon made himself the all-powerful emperor.

In the summer of 1805 Bolivar met up with Rodriguez, his old tutor from Venezuela. They embarked on a walking tour of Italy, carrying their packs on their backs, sleeping in haystacks, enjoying the outdoors, and discussing endlessly the ideas of the great European thinkers. Inspired by Rodriguez, Bolivar made his famous promise: "I swear before you, I swear before the God of my fathers…that I shall not rest until I have broken the chains that oppress us." From then on, Bolivar dedicated his efforts to the independence of his homeland of Venezuela.

One day after Bolivar had returned to his estates in Venezuela, he was invited to a formal reception at the Spanish governor's palace. He was very aware of the tremors of independence that were moving up and down Latin America, inspired by the American example of self-rule to the north, including two unsuccessful revolts within Venezuela. At the reception he reportedly took his turn at offering a toast, saying, "I also raise my glass for the happiness of the king, but I lift it even higher for the independence of all Spanish America." He wasn't arrested on the spot, but the governor was furious and Bolivar's every subsequent move was watched.

In 1808 a sudden turn of events in Europe brought the break from Spain. Napoleon had taken the Spanish crown by force, putting his French brother on the throne of Spain. Thrown into a state of turmoil, the claim of Spain over its colonies in Latin America began to crack, and the wars of independence in the Spanish colonies began.

In the capital city of Caracas, the Creoles of Venezuela made their Spanish rulers step down and put their own people in charge. Bolivar was made a colonel in the army. The commander of the army was General Francisco de Miranda, who had led the earlier unsuccessful revolts. In 1811 the First Congress of Venezuela was formed and the group declared that Venezuela was a republic independent from Spain. Declaring independence and maintaining it are two very different things, however, and the fight to remove Spanish control continued for twelve years. Spain was loath to give up such a valuable prize as Venezuela, plus there were many Venezuelans, especially Creoles, who remained loyal to Spain and fought against the revolutionary forces led by Miranda, and later by Bolivar.

In 1813, after two years of fighting, Bolivar led his army into Caracas in triumph, and the city council declared him "El Libertador," the Liberator of Venezuela. But the war was far from over, for royal armies were still in control of other parts of the country. As a Creole, Bolivar represented the privileged class, and the slaves and poor people did not trust him. Instead, in increasing numbers, they joined the Spaniards on the royalist side. Control of the country shifted back and forth between the revolutionaries and the royalists as the war continued.

In May 1819 General Bolivar led his troops in a daring and decisive move. According to the reports of his spies, the Spanish had few soldiers remaining in the area called New Granada, located just south of present day Panama at the northernmost point of South America. Bolivar took a huge gamble and led his army of more than 2000 men through the Orinoco River's jungles during the rainy season to invade New Granada. For a week straight the soldiers marched in water that was from waist to chest-high, infested with deadly boa constrictors and crocodiles up to twenty feet in length. After that ordeal, they faced crossing the windy, snow-covered Andes Mountains. Bolivar pushed his army on, even though some died in the snowy mountain passes. The Spanish troops were taken by surprise, and the independence of New Granada was securely established. Bolivar was honored as a hero and cheered by the people as El Libertador.

In was not until June 1821 that Bolivar's army finally ousted the Spanish army from Venezuelan soil. Wild with joy, the people celebrated their freedom with parades in Bolivar's honor. Further fighting continued until the end of 1824 when all of South America was finally free from Spanish control. Upper Peru changed its name to Bolivia, in honor of their liberator. Six present-day countries were freed from Spanish control: Venezuela, Colombia, Panama, Ecuador, Peru and Bolivia. After twelve years of war and upheaval, Bolivar had finally fulfilled his youthful promise to break the chains of servitude in his homeland.

Bolivar's final years were not easy. As the president of Venezuela, New Granada, Ecuador, Peru and Bolivia, he had many difficulties governing, and his hope of creating a permanent confederation of South American nations was not realized. There were frequent plots to overthrow his rule, both from abroad and from disgruntled nationalists. In 1828 he survived an assassination attempt by fleeing through a bedroom window and hiding under a bridge overnight with his pastry chef.

On a happier note, he fell in love once again, this time with a woman of a very different style. Manuela Saenz de Thorne rode a horse and could shoot a gun. Unlike any woman he had ever met, she did not hesitate to stand her ground in any argument and, being extremely well-read, she could often prove her point by quoting an authoritative source. Even Manuela's friendship could not save Bolivar from the illness of tuberculosis and moods of depression that characterized his last years. He died on December 17, 1830, at age 47.

Although he had fallen from favor at the end of his lifetime, in later years people in the countries that he had liberated honored his accomplishments by naming cities, streets, schools and parks after him. A man of great ambition, he had fought to bring freedom to his people and then died uncertain that they would maintain the hard-fought freedoms that he had worked so hard to achieve.

Benito Juárez
(1806–1872)

Significance: Mexican president and national hero, Benito Juárez worked to build a nation while warring with foreign invaders, primarily France. He was the first indigenous national to serve as President of Mexico, which he did for five terms.

Benito Juárez was born on March 21, 1806, in a small village of twenty Zapotec (American/Indian) families near the town of Oaxaca, about 250 miles southwest of Mexico City. Although the area was remote and barely influenced by the Spanish rule, the Catholic Church was a strong presence. Juárez was baptized in a nearby church by his father, godmother and grandparents. The strength of the extended family was essential in his upbringing, because by the time Juárez was three years old, both of his parents had died and he and his two older sisters moved to the house of their grandparents. They, in turn, died within a few short years, and the

Juárez children lived with a changing circle of relatives and friends who looked after their welfare and education. It is hard to imagine how it came about, but much later Juárez recalled that he had bought his uncle the whip to be used when he had not studied his lessons with sufficient diligence. He was not a very motivated student at home; the stimulation of the city was what intrigued him.

According to stories told about him, he was tending his uncle's sheep and some passing soldiers talked him into giving them some of the sheep, perhaps in exchange for some money. To avoid punishment and seek adventure, he headed to the state capital where one of his older sisters was working as a maid. Her employer, Antonio Maza, who was probably a European, took an interest in Juárez and put him into school at the seminary where, as a full-blooded Zapotec, he was allowed to study for free. Maza's expectation was that Juárez would continue on to become a priest.

Short and stocky in stature, Juárez matured into a handsome, commanding figure with dark hair, large eyes, a strong, straight nose and a firm but wide and full mouth. He was also forming a mind and voice of his own. At age fifteen, his Latin studies at the school were completed, but he refused to begin the steps for entering priesthood. Even at this early age, he had developed a negative attitude toward the pervasive role of the Church in Mexican governmental affairs. The friction between church and state continued to be a divisive theme in Mexican society during his lifetime.

Juárez was also aware that as a Zapotec, he would be trained only just enough to be able to lead the illiterate faithful in prayer, but he would never be given any opportunities for advancement within the Church.

Because he now wanted to continue his studies and a non-religious school had opened, Juárez enrolled and eventually earned a law degree. Studying in Oaxaca, he and fellow students could envision the fulfillment of a national heritage that was based on Indian culture rather than foreign Spanish. Being away from Mexico City where the European influence was strong, young students in Oaxaca were able to form a unified sense of Mexico's Indian identity. To this day, Mexico remains a mixed culture whose people are three-tenths Indian, six-tenths mixed (mestizo) and one tenth European (primarily Spanish). Indians like Juárez, who typically have darker skin, have always had to work harder to gain opportunities and advantages in jobs and society in general.

Juárez's legal and political career advanced, and he often represented cases that challenged the status quo of the Church in political situations. For example, he had a case in which his clients were claiming that they had been overcharged for religious services. Standing just over five feet tall and wearing a black suit, he had a reputation for thoroughness and toughness. He was appointed a judge and later president of the provincial court. In 1847 he was elected governor of the state of Oaxaca and was one of the delegates to gather in Mexico City to revise the national constitution.

In 1855 Juárez took part in the revolution that overthrew Santa Ana, the Mexican military general who had seized the national government two years earlier. As minister of justice in the new government, he instituted a series of liberal reforms that were a major influence on the laws of modern Mexico. Special privileges for the military and the Church were among the most serious abuses he wanted to stamp out. He established a law that led to the breakup of the Church's great landholdings allowing sale to tenants. Juárez helped write the Constitution of 1857, which sought finally to separate church and state and establish public schools. Then Juárez returned to Oaxaca, where he was again elected governor with nine of every ten votes cast.

As he wrestled with the country's problems, his personal life was marred with its share of heartache. He married Margarita, the daughter of his benefactor, Maza, when he was 37 and she was just 17. She was quoted as saying later, "He is very homely but very good." He had two illegitimate children before their marriage, a son with whom he maintained contact and a daughter who became a drug addict and whose care he provided for through relatives. Twelve children were born to Juárez and Margarita. The death of his two-year-old daughter, Guadalupe, was a terrible blow.

In 1857 Juárez was elected to the nation's second highest position. A revolt broke out when Comonfort, the president, tried to seize supreme power, and Mexico fell into a period of civil war. Juárez represented constitutional government, but as the weaker force, he had to flee the capital and stay on the move. The Church and more conservative forces were against him; the Indians and liberal groups supported him. He fled to Veracruz where he set up a new seat of government in opposition until 1860 when he was able to bring his constitutionally-elected presidency back to Mexico City.

Facing the financial disaster caused by nearly five years of civil war, Juárez suspended debt repayments to foreign creditors including Britain, Spain and France. In response, in December 1861 and January 1862, the British landed 700 marines, the Spanish 6000 troops, and the French 250 soldiers on the eastern coast. Juárez, in a gentlemanly if misguided gesture, gave permission to the invading troops to move inland away from the scourge of yellow fever along the swampy coast. Juárez reached a settlement with Britain and Spain, so they withdrew their troops.

On May 5, a date that remains a proud symbol of Mexican history, the Battle of Puebla (on the road to Mexico City) was fought, and the French were defeated, at least briefly. For the next four years, French arrogance would cause 40,000 Mexicans to be killed in the ensuing fighting. With Juárez and his government driven into internal exile, Napoleon III, in an effort to prove himself an equal to his famous uncle, dispatched Maximilian, his Austrian puppet, to be crowned emperor of Mexico. With the backing of some Mexican conservatives, Maximilian was proclaimed Maximilian I of Mexico on April 10, 1864. Juárez moved his constitutionally-elected government to the north and continued military resistance against the French forces. Before Juárez fled, Congress granted him an emergency extension of his presidency.

Maximilian's government had numerous difficulties. One problem was the inferior number of troops he commanded; they were 35,000 strong, but Mexico is a huge country. Porfirio Diaz, an opposition commander loyal to Juárez's government, was an exceptionally competent commander and was causing Maximilian's forces considerable grief. In addition, Maximilian issued proclamations that infuriated the Church where his most royalist sympathizers resided. The last major battle was Queretaro, where Maximilian's forces numbered 9000, but the republican forces numbered three times that. Maximilian was captured trying to escape at night. Imprisoned, he sent a message to Juárez asking for a meeting, but Juárez replied that he could have his say at the trial. The trial took place in a theater, and Maximilian refused to attend. A seven-member panel voted: three to banish and four to execute. On June 19, 1867, on the hill where he'd been captured, Maximilian and his two top officers faced a firing squad as 4000 Mexican soldiers watched.

Juárez returned to Mexico City and was reelected president. His wife arrived with their five unmarried daughters and young Benito, their only surviving son. She also brought the remains of their two other sons who had died while she was in exile in the United States. The family moved into a hotel rather than the national palace.

The task of rebuilding the country was overwhelming, and Juárez was forced to be satisfied with minor victories. He suffered a stroke in October 1870, and his beloved Margarita died in their small house a few months later at the age of 42. Juárez invited no one to her secular funeral, but respectful crowds lined the streets anyway. In 1872, leaving his office complaining of chest pains, he went home where he died, attended by one servant. The next uprising, led by Porfirio Diaz, was already forming. Mexico's "Age of the Indian" was ended.

FREDERICK DOUGLASS
(CIRCA 1817–1895)

Significance: Once a slave himself, he was the most prominent abolitionist leader in the U.S. and brought international attention to the anti-slavery movement.

No one knows for certain when Frederick Douglass was born. He was just another slave boy, and no one could predict that he would one day become the best known black man in the country. Until he was eight years old, life was hard. He didn't see his mother, Harriet Bailey, very much. When he was just a week old, she was ordered back to work some distance away, and his grandmother was given the task of looking after him. At age six, Frederick's grandmother told him they were taking a journey together, and as they set out, he clung to her skirts in fear and uncertainty. They arrived at a large plantation, and his grandmother pointed out three children working in the field who were his estranged older siblings. She told him to join his brother and two sisters, which he did very reluctantly, and not long after he looked up to see that his grandmother had gone without a goodbye. He threw himself to the ground and wept.

The harsh realities of the slave system were a lesson he quickly learned. Like other slave children, he had to work long hours running errands, working in the fields and doing household jobs. Hunger was a constant companion, and the slave children were fed cornmeal mush that was placed in a trough, to which they were called like livestock. They used homemade spoons from oyster shells to eat with and fought over every last scrap of food. At night Frederick slept on a damp earth floor with a blanket made from flour sacks. The cook at the plantation, also a slave, gave him frequent beatings.

At age eight, Frederick was sent to Baltimore, Maryland, to live with his master's relatives, Sophia and Hugh Auld, who had a son about Frederick's age. Suddenly he was eating decent food, wearing good clothing and enjoying proper treatment. Best of all, as Mrs. Auld taught her son to read and write, she included Frederick in the lessons, even though it was illegal to educate blacks. Eventually Mr. Auld discovered that his wife had taught Frederick to read and write, and the lessons stopped abruptly. Slave owners believed that if slaves became educated, they would begin to think for themselves and not obey their owners' orders. Although his lessons ended, Frederick did not stop reading at every possible opportunity. He was often sent on errands where he met poor white boys who were short on food, and because they attended school and had access to books while he had access to food, he sometimes traded food for reading lessons.

As a teenager, Frederick grew tall and strong with a large nose, thick eyebrows, flashing eyes and a mass of wiry hair. When he was sixteen, his owner died and he was sold in the same way as the family's other property. Back on a farm again, he was beaten and nearly starved again. His independent spirit got him in constant trouble as he refused to bend to the will of his new owner, so he was sent to a slave breaker named Edward Covey. For nearly a year, Covey tried to cure Frederick's independent streak with brutal floggings with a leather strap. One day Frederick saw his opportunity, and he grabbed Covey by the throat and they fought viciously until both of them lay exhausted on the ground. After that encounter, Frederick did not gain his freedom, but he at least had earned Covey's respect, and they kept their distance.

It was only a matter of time until he ran away. He made more than one attempt before he was successful. His escape came when he borrowed identification papers, called free papers, from a free friend and boarded a train for New York City. He feared that the papers would be checked closely and he would be discovered, but his luck held out. In New York he changed his name to Frederick Augustus Douglass, and he soon married Anna Murray, a free black girl he had fallen in love with. The happy couple moved to New Bedford, Massachusetts, to start a new life.

He had to take whatever job he could find, and he worked in a shipyard loading cargo while his wife took in laundry and mending. Very soon Frederick joined the abolitionists who were working to end slavery, and he stumbled on the discovery that he had a gift for speaking to audiences. He had a splendid, persuasive voice, and as he spoke about his slavery days, people leaned forward to listen, enraptured by his words. Standing well over six feet tall, he was a handsome figure whose strong jaw and piercing eyes captured people's attention. As he described his slave days, he sent chills down the spines of his listeners.

He was given a job by the abolitionists to travel throughout the New England states, to speak out against slavery in churches and at community gatherings. Even though he was in the North where many people sympathized with the blacks, he still was forced to ride in railroad cars designated "For Colored Only." There was so much interest in his story that he wrote an autobiography that was read even by people in the South. Since he was a runaway slave, the book and his public speaking made him a target for slave catchers. To avoid capture, he traveled to England where he was treated on an equal level such as he had never experienced before. Before he returned to the United States, friends purchased his freedom for him for the price of $711.

Back in the U.S. the Douglasses moved to Rochester, New York, where they joined the Underground Railroad network and provided a stopping place for runaways heading for Canada. He also started a weekly newspaper, *The North Star,* named to remind himself and others of the journey north when slaves followed the North Star to guide them. Frederick continued to write articles, give speeches and meet with leaders of the antislavery societies.

In 1859 there was a difficult event involving the white abolitionist, John Brown, who was planning an uprising against slave owners that would involve guns and killing. He tried to persuade Frederick Douglass to join, and the two strong-willed men argued for two days. Frederick was torn, but he chose not to join a plan that not only would mean violence, but that he believed was also doomed due to a lack of enough participants and inadequate resources. Finally they parted, John Brown to die for black people's freedom and Frederick Douglass to live for it and work on.

In November 1860 Abraham Lincoln was elected president, and the Civil War began one and a half years later. Frederick Douglass recognized that the war represented a way to freedom for the blacks if the North won, so he encouraged them to join the Northern armies. His own two sons were quick to join, and eventually nearly 200,000 blacks served. Some 36,000 blacks were killed in action.

Later Douglass discovered that black soldiers were receiving only half the pay of whites, and when he met with President Lincoln to give advice, he pushed for equal pay. The two men respected each other, and after Lincoln's untimely death in 1865, his wife sent Douglass the president's favorite walking stick.

In Douglass's final years, he kept up his activities on behalf of his people. His bushy white hair, well-shaped beard and proud bearing were a distinct and well known sight. He worked for voting rights, education and fair treatment for blacks. He spoke against the separation of blacks and whites in restaurants, trains and other public places. He also voiced support for women's voting rights, spoke out against mistreatment of Chinese immigrants and American Indians, and worked for better schools for all. On February 20, 1895, the last day of his life, he spoke to a large gathering in Washington, D.C., concerning women's suffrage.

HARRIET TUBMAN
(1820–1913)

Significance: Leader of the Underground Railroad during the abolitionist period just prior to the Civil War, she continued working for the rights of black Americans as well as women's rights.

Harriet Tubman might have been born a slave, but she was determined not to die a slave. She not only won her own freedom, but by risking her life many times, she was responsible for the freedom of hundreds of other slaves. During the Civil War years, Harriet served her country as a spy, nurse and scout. She repeatedly provided for the needs of others, and by the time she died at age 93, she was a famous and respected American who was known for her efforts to establish the rights of blacks and women.

It is not known exactly when Harriet was born, so the year 1820 is approximate. Her grandparents had been captured in West Africa and forced into slavery, and her parents were born as slaves in the U.S. Originally named Araminta Ross, she was one of eleven children born to Harriet Greene and Benjamin Ross on a plantation near Bucktown, Maryland. She later adopted her mother's name.

By age five she was already working as a maid and babysitter for the plantation owner's baby. When the baby cried, Harriet was whipped. One day she was lashed five times before breakfast. Another time she was accused of stealing a lump of sugar, and she hid in the neighbor's pig sty for five days, fighting with the pigs for scraps of food, just to avoid more punishment. When she was six, she learned to weave and make clothes. By age twelve, she labored in the fields of corn, potatoes and tobacco. Harriet was strong and good at her work, but she barely held her rebellious nature in check. When she angered the overseer, she received severe beatings.

When she was thirteen, such a beating left her seriously injured. It happened when Harriet refused to help the overseer hold a man down for a beating. The overseer reacted furiously toward her, and in the confusing scene that followed, the man tried to run away. The overseer tried to stop him, and Harriet purposely got in the way. The overseer hit her with a heavy weight, originally intended for the male slave, and she collapsed with a skull injury. Later she said that her hair probably saved her life because it had never been combed and stood out like a thicket. The blow left her with permanent neurological damage, and for the rest of her life she experienced sudden blackouts. She never could predict when one would happen or how long it would last. She would just wake up suddenly and go on, feeling as though nothing had happened.

After she recovered enough to return to work, she went back to the fields: plowing, planting, hoeing and chopping wood. Because of her physical strength, she did the same work as most men. During this time she learned about the woods from her father, and this knowledge would prove important to her later on.

When Harriet was in her early twenties, she received permission from her master to marry John Tubman, a free black man who lived near the plantation. For the next five years, she continued to work as a slave but she was allowed to live in her husband's cabin. It was an uncertain time, because as a slave she could be sold at any moment to a plantation far away. After the plantation owner died, rumors were flying that the slaves would all be sold to settle the estate. Rather than be sold, Harriet decided that she would escape to the North where slavery was not allowed. Saying it was too dangerous, John Tubman refused to accompany her, and so she made her escape plans in secret without him. She started out with two of her brothers, but they both turned back because they were afraid they would be caught.

Filled with a mixture of fear and determination, Harriet went on alone. She had directions to the house of a woman who would help her on the journey, but there was no way to be certain that she was not walking into a trap. It turned out that the woman was a part of the network of sympathizers known as the Underground Railroad who moved runaway slaves north by hiding them in wagons under burlap sacks of supplies. Harriet walked much of the way, following back roads and remote paths through the woods by night with the North Star to keep her oriented in the right direction. Traveling a distance of almost one hundred miles, always fearing detection, Harriet walked to freedom in Pennsylvania. In Philadelphia she got a job washing dishes, and for the first time in her life, she experienced the pleasures of being paid for her work, living in her own place, and being able to go wherever she wanted.

In Philadelphia, Harriet Tubman joined the abolitionist cause with others who were working to end slavery. She decided to become a "conductor" on the Underground Railroad and help other slaves escape from the South. In 1850 she decided to return to Maryland and escort her own family to freedom. She also hoped to persuade John Tubman to join her, but as it turned out, he had remarried during her absence. She returned to the same plantation where she had lived, and her sister and her children accompanied her north on her first trip. Over a period of ten years she made nineteen trips and escorted approximately 300 slaves to the North, including one of her brothers and her aged parents.

Large rewards were offered for her capture, but she was never caught. One of her clever methods of avoiding detection involved using disguises. For example, she could impersonate an old half-crazy man to throw off authorities on her trail. Another trick was to pour pepper on the trail to confuse dogs that were tracking the runaways. Another technique was to hide near home until the people who were looking for them thought they were long gone and gave up looking. Then the journey would begin.

Harriet maintained strict rules as a conductor. Once she started north with a group of passengers, no one was allowed to turn back. Anyone who turned back might very well be caught and forced to give away the location of the other runaways. Even though she never had to use it, Harriet carried a gun to enforce strict discipline that she deemed necessary for the safety of the group. A crying baby could also be a hazard for a group trying to avoid detection, so Harriet carried a sleeping powder for that purpose. Most slaves, including Harriet, made their escape on Saturday nights. They chose this timing because most slaves did not work on Sundays, and thus might not be missed until Monday morning.

There were many close calls. In one situation with an amusing twist, Harriet and her passengers were near a train station, intending to board going northward. Some slave hunters were close behind them, and Harriet managed to save her group by pushing them onto a different train that was heading south. The trick worked perfectly, and the slave hunters ignored them since they were traveling in the "wrong" direction.

Harriet never lost any of her charges and had an uncanny ability of avoiding danger on these hazardous trips. Among escaped slaves, she became known as Moses, after the Bible story of Moses leading the Hebrew people out of slavery in Egypt. By 1860, Harriet was well known for her daring slave rescues, and she was often invited to speak against slavery at northern abolitionist rallies. Although illness prevented her from being present, she supported John Brown in his ill-fated rebellion against slavery at Harper's Ferry.

During the Civil War it was a difficult decision to leave her elderly parents living in New York State, but the cause of the Union was too important to Harriet. Her years of surviving in the woods and swamps made her a valuable spy for the Northern army, and she often went behind enemy lines to gain information from the slaves there. In 1863 she led a regiment of black soldiers, known as the Glory Brigade, on a raid in South Carolina.

Harriet was later praised for her service during the war, but there was no pay to help her with the mounting debts of her parents' living expenses. Luckily, a friend named Sarah Bradford helped her by writing and publishing her biography, *Scenes from the Life of Harriet Tubman*. The book told of her work with the Underground Railroad, and its popularity provided some modest, much needed, income.

In 1870 Harriet married Nelson Davis, a former slave, whom she had met during the war while guiding the Glory Brigade. They were together for eighteen years until his death. The U.S. government began giving her twenty dollars each month, starting in 1897, not for the work she had done during the war but because it had been owed to her husband, who had been a soldier. Only after she died did she receive full honors from the military. As a tribute for all her important work during the Civil War, she was buried with the ceremony usually reserved for soldiers.

ELIZABETH CADY STANTON
(1815–1902)

Significance: Until the 19th century, women were not allowed to vote and held very few legal rights. Along with Susan B. Anthony, Elizabeth Cady Stanton led the struggle for women's suffrage.

Elizabeth Cady was born on November 12, 1815, in Johnstown, New York, the fourth of six children. Her mother gave birth to eleven children, but five of her siblings died in infancy. Elizabeth's brother Eleazar died at age twenty just prior to his graduation from college, so only Elizabeth and her four sisters lived into adulthood and old age.

Elizabeth's father, Daniel Cady, was a prominent attorney who, during his career, served as a U.S. Congressman, a circuit court judge and a New York Supreme Court justice. Through her father, Elizabeth was exposed to the study of law, and her interest in temperance and the antislavery movement began early. As a young girl in her teens, she enjoyed lively conversations and debates over legal issues with her father's law clerks. It was this early exposure to the law that caused her to see how the law favored men so much over women. Married women were in a worse situation than single women; they possessed no rights for property, income, employment, or even custody over their own children.

Stanton's mother, Margaret Livingston Cady, was a tall woman with a commanding, even queenly presence, but the loss of so many children caused her to suffer periods of depression, which kept her from being fully involved in the lives of her surviving children. Judge Cady coped with this loss by devoting himself to his work.

As many Northern families of the time, the Cadys owned a slave, Peter Teabout, who took care of Elizabeth and her sisters. He later became a freeman. In her memoir Stanton wrote fondly about attending church with Teabout and enjoying the chance to sit in the back of the church with him rather than in the front with the other white families of the congregation.

Although Stanton never went to college, she was formally educated beyond the norm for young women at that time. As a young teen, she studied Latin, Greek and mathematics, winning honors and awards for her performances. She also experienced being in co-educational classes where she could compete with boys her age and older. Upon graduation from secondary school, Stanton experienced a strong dose of sexual discrimination as she watched the young men in her class continue on into a college that barred women.

When Stanton's brother died at age 20, her father was devastated at losing his only son. She tried to comfort her father, saying that she would try to be all her brother would have been, but her father's disheartening response upset her: "Oh, my daughter, I wish you were a boy!" The fact that boys were valued more than girls was to become a life theme.

The existing photos of her in young adulthood show warm, friendly eyes, a round face and thick, brown hair pulled loosely back in a bun. Her clothing was stylish, and she wore fashionable hats and bonnets with her long, wide dresses. As she aged and experienced childbearing, her figure expanded to a pleasantly plump shape, and she took to wearing carefully curled ringlets in her white hair.

As a young woman, Stanton spent time at the house of her cousin who was an abolitionist, and there she met her future husband, Henry Brewster Stanton, a journalist and abolitionist orator. Despite the reservations of Elizabeth's father, they married in 1840.

For their honeymoon the Stantons traveled to Europe, including a stay in London to attend the World Anti-slavery Convention. Elizabeth's future activism got a boost when she discovered that women delegates were not allowed to speak. Relegated to the upper gallery, she met an outraged Lucretia Mott, and Stanton recalled later, "As Mrs. Mott and I walked home, arm in arm, commenting on the incidents of the day, we resolved to hold a convention as soon as we returned home and form a society to advocate the rights of women."

Following their honeymoon, Elizabeth and Henry moved into her parents' household. Henry studied law under his father-in-law for three years, and then the couple moved to Boston where Henry joined a law firm. In Boston Elizabeth was engaged in a constant round of abolitionist gatherings, and during this time she enjoyed the company of influential people such as Frederick Douglass, Louisa May Alcott and Ralph Waldo Emerson. She spent her early married life in a charming house surrounded by sympathetic friends and assisted by two hardworking servants. She was stout, fond of fancy dresses, and anchored to her responsibilities as a wife and mother. Loving a clean, orderly home, she couldn't understand why every woman didn't love housework. She gave the man who delivered her firewood a tip to pile the logs with the smooth ends outward in a perfect stack.

During her lifetime it was virtually unheard of that a married woman would not adopt the usual custom of being addressed as the wife of her husband, in her case, Mrs. Henry B. Stanton. She took her husband's surname as part of her own and signed her name Elizabeth Cady Stanton, maintaining the Cady name, but she refused to be addressed as Mrs. Henry B. Stanton. When they took their wedding vows, Elizabeth refused to include the words "to obey," agreeing instead to treating him as an equal.

Although the couple shared similar temperament and ambitions, Henry Stanton disagreed with his wife's views on women's rights, leading to tension and disagreement at times. Nevertheless, the marriage lasted for 47 years, ending with Henry's death in 1887.

The Stantons had seven children, the last child born when Elizabeth was 44. Her views on childbearing were unique at the time. She asserted that her children were conceived under a plan of "voluntary motherhood," and she strongly held that women should have control over their sexuality and childbearing. For her children she advocated plenty of outdoor activity, homeopathic medicine and a highly academic education.

The convention for women's rights with Lucretia Mott was eight years in coming. The Stantons had moved to an unromantic mill town in upstate New York, and the novelty of housekeeping had passed away. Lucretia Mott came for a visit, and fired with sudden enthusiasm, they wrote up a newspaper announcement calling for a women's rights convention to be held five days later. They drafted a "Womanifesto" modeled after the Declaration of Independence and found a Methodist church where the sessions could be held. On the appointed day, to everyone's surprise, the roads to the church were crowded with wagons and carriages. Even forty men showed up in support, and the women quickly dropped plans to exclude males. In fact, because women were so unaccustomed to speaking in public before crowds, Mott's husband was asked to preside.

For the first time Stanton spoke in public. There were complaints later that she spoke too softly to be heard. In her short speech she called for the right to vote, which even most of the women present thought was demanding too much too fast. Her husband left town when he heard what his wife was proposing. Her father—who had hurried over to check for signs of insanity in his daughter—threatened to disinherit her. The convention was covered in the national newspapers, generally with derisive scorn, and most of the women who had signed the "Womanifesto" meekly withdrew their names.

Despite the rocky beginning, the women's movement had been born and new energy was drawn to the cause. Two weeks later there was another convention held in a nearby town with Quakers, freethinkers and restless housewives in attendance. Stanton barely managed to attend because she had difficulty getting a babysitter.

No one knows exactly how Elizabeth Cady Stanton and Susan B. Anthony first became friends, but it was a small world of people who believed in women's rights before the Civil War. Their talents were an ideal match. Stanton was the idea person who wrote speeches and newspaper articles and pushed Anthony to expand the reformist platform to include the issues of divorce reform and religion. She never worried about shocking people, and on her eightieth birthday she announced to her audience that it was time to rewrite the Bible. Anthony, on the other hand, was the worker bee type, happy to be traveling to every corner of the country to carry the message.

Both women were dedicated to the cause of the abolitionists—ending slavery—and they spent the

Civil War years collecting signatures on petitions, campaigning and lobbying. They naively assumed that it would naturally follow that once African American men got the vote, women's suffrage would be the next obvious step. They were bitterly angry that semi-literate black men would get the vote before educated white women, and a split arose in the women's movement, leaving radical feminists like Anthony and Stanton on one side and the more moderate women on the other.

By the turn of century Stanton and Anthony, the two great suffrage warriors, were resigned to the reality that they would not live to see women have the vote. Although they worked tirelessly for the cause, and there were increasingly locations that allowed women to vote on local issues such as the school board, there were endless frustrating delays on the national level. Stanton and Anthony watched while other countries passed up the United States in granting enfranchisement to women. At age 86, Stanton bemoaned, "Our movement is belated and, like all things too long postponed, gets on everybody's nerves."

In 1920, eighteen years after her death, the 19th Amendment to the U.S. Constitution was finally passed, giving U.S. women the vote. Fellow 19th-century activist Susan B. Anthony might have more name recognition, as well as her own dollar coin, but even she acknowledged Stanton as the true founder of the women's rights movement.

Postscript: Why was there such lengthy resistance to the women's vote? Most of the talk was about keeping women safe at home, but in reality they were already in the work place in many areas. The real reasons were more practical. Democrats suspected that women would vote Republican. Women were suspected to be soft on reform movements. The liquor industry knew women were against their interests. Southern politicians were solidly against women's enfranchisement; they had maneuvered the vote away from black men by the end of the century, and the last thing they wanted was pressure to allow black women the vote.

CLARA BARTON
(1841–1912)

Significance: Barton's biography is one perspective on the Civil War experience. Additionally, her story offers a glimpse into two other topics: early modern medicine and the role of women in 19th century American society.

Clara Barton was born on Christmas Day in 1841 on a farm near Boston. She was of a strong but slender build with quiet, observant eyes and dark brown hair that she wore parted in the middle and pulled back or fastened on top of her head as she grew older. She wore long dresses with high necklines, often trimmed in white, with a tight waist and a row of buttons down the front.

There were pleasant periods in her early childhood, but there was also a dark side to family life. Her mother suffered from mental illness, and her behavior was irrational at times. The parents argued a great deal. Clara's older sister Dolly also suffered from serious mental illness, and when she was uncontrollable, she was locked in her room and howled for hours. Clara had two brothers and one other sister who were all free from the curse that afflicted their mother and sister Dolly.

Clara acquired a reputation as an extremely shy person, and it seems very possible that the cause for her timidity was the squabbling between her parents and other friction in the household surrounding her sister Dolly. She also developed a stubborn streak and enjoyed outdoor activities such as horseback riding, ice skating and dancing. Girls were not allowed to be active in the way boys were, and she resented it. For example, girls who rode horses were expected to ride only sidesaddle, but Clara defied the rule whenever she could.

Like other girls, she learned to cook, sew, weave on a loom and do other household tasks. A few mills and factories were springing up in the area, but nearly everything was still done by hand. Clothes were washed on a large washtub with a washboard, and cooking was done on stoves heated with chunks of chopped wood. Hard work was taken for granted as the way of life.

To cure her of shyness, Clara's parents sent her away to a boarding school at age eleven, but she was soon sent home when she lost her appetite and quit eating. Her first nursing experience came when her grown brother David was seriously injured by falling off the roof of the barn. At the time using leeches to draw blood was accepted medical practice, so David's treatment caused his illness to stretch out for two years until the bloodletting was stopped. Clara tended her brother during this time, and the nursing experience was a valuable education for her. On the other hand, being so occupied with her brother's care did not provide her with much chance to overcome her shyness.

After her brother recovered, her parents encouraged her to try teaching, and as it turned out, she was very successful at it. Once she used her riding whip on an unruly student, and after that, she had no discipline trouble! She gained confidence in herself and became popular with her pupils and admired by the headmaster. By age thirty her growing ambition to do more dramatic work led her to seek a different type of position, this time in Washington, D.C., which seemed the place for larger tasks.

Once inn Washington, D.C., Clara Barton dismissed the idea of returning to teaching; she was looking for something where she could play a bigger role. Although there was prejudice against women in almost all other jobs, she used family connections to gain a position as a personal secretary to the head of the Patent Office where she witnessed how to connect with men in powerful positions. Not everyone was tolerant of having a woman in a government office, and she occasionally endured nasty jokes and gossip. Even when cigar smoke was blown in her face, she toughed it out. As a Patent Office worker in Washington, she was paid the same salary as the men, although the commissioner in charge was afraid to let anyone in Congress know.

The year was 1854, and tensions were rising between the Northern and Southern states over slavery. The Northern position was increasingly anti-slavery, and that made the Southerners all that much more determined to keep their slaves. Increasingly, Southerners were taking the position that the Southern states should split off from the Union and form their own government. Not all Southerners wanted to secede from the Union, but the separatist leaders were fervent about their cause. Abraham Lincoln was elected president in 1860, and his declared priority was to keep the Union whole, even if it meant allowing slavery to continue where it already existed.

Tensions between the states intensified, with more and more Southern states seceding. In April 1861 the state of South Carolina began the actual war by having their militia attack Fort Sumter, a Union stronghold on an island in the harbor of Charleston, SC. The Union troops were overwhelmed and forced to surrender. Four days later the Sixth Massachusetts Regiment, one of the first Northern groups to be called up to fight, marched south to defend Washington, D.C., and as they traveled through Maryland, Southern sympathizers attacked, wounding thirty and killing three. Clara was shocked to discover many of her former students among the wounded and killed.

Nearly forty young men who had been Clara Barton's students were in the Sixth Massachusetts

Regiment, and she rushed to give aid and be of service. The wounded men were temporarily housed in the chambers of the U.S. Senate, and Clara quickly became a point person for their families sending food and clothing to "her boys." She was nearly overwhelmed with the boxes of lovingly packed parcels.

The lack of medical supplies and personnel was a dire situation. The shortage of makeshift field hospitals was a crisis, and even those that existed lacked basic supplies such as bandages. Modern medicine was at its beginning, and the importance of hygiene in preventing infections was unknown. By using surgical instruments without sterilizing them, doctors unwittingly added to the misery. Most of the wounded died, sometimes from infection, but also from dehydration and exposure. When trains carrying the wounded arrived at hospitals, the passengers were a mass of dead and living mixed together. Anyone who was inclined to help and had a strong stomach could find a place to help. Clara lost little time in deciding that caring for the wounded soldiers was her new calling.

Barton had many contacts, so when she began asking for supplies and donations, she was flooded with things such as preserves, soap and lemons to prevent scurvy. Within a few short months she had filled three warehouses with supplies to be taken to the military hospitals. At first she took supplies to meet the trains bringing back the wounded, but then she realized that she needed to find a way to get supplies directly to the battlefield. Although it was against military regulations, her deliveries were so desperately needed that before long she was receiving unofficial leaks of information indicating which trauma centers were the next priority. Military officers were hesitant to allow her to go to the front, but Clara was able to talk her way past them because she could deliver desperately needed food, bandages, tobacco, medicines and even liquor from her warehouses.

Clara spent a great deal of her time sending out appeals for supplies and organizing them, but she preferred to be on the battlefields in the thick of the action where she soon earned a reputation for bravery. At times her skin was stained blue from gunpowder and her skirt edges were crusty with dried blood. Once she was crossing a bridge during heavy fire, and an exploding shell tore away a large chunk of her heavy skirt. When there were too many wounded at one battle for the few doctors available, she stepped up and removed a bullet from a soldier's face while another injured soldier gripped his head to hold him still.

A lot of people were shocked at the thought that women like Clara Barton were going into hospitals and even onto battlefields where they were bound to see dreadful sights and hear uncouth language. But these nurses were saving the lives of many soldiers, and before long they were getting positive publicity, even being called "angels of the battlefield." These volunteer nurses became crucial in dealing with the large numbers of broken limbs, serious wounds and rapidly spreading diseases in the hospital camps.

One of the bloodiest battles of the Civil War was at Antietam where nearly 5000 men died and over 18,000 were wounded in just a few hours. Clara knew in advance that the battle at Antietam was approaching, and she wanted to be in on the action. She arrived with her supply wagon stocked with bandages and medicines even as the firing was still going on. As the shooting continued, she delivered soup to tired and hungry men, bandaging the wounded and offering comfort to the dying. The sight of her on the battlefield cheered the men, and the Union army officials came to see the great value she had in boosting morale. Stories of Clara Barton appeared in newspapers and thousands of soldiers knew her. Although her boldness rubbed some people the wrong way, she was better known to Americans than many of the generals in the Civil War.

The North claimed Antietam as a victory, albeit a slim one, and Abraham Lincoln was emboldened to issue the Emancipation Proclamation that led to the end of slavery.

When the Civil War ended, President Lincoln commissioned Barton to head up a comprehensive search for missing soldiers, and she ran a government office that eventually tracked down information on over 20,000 soldiers. Then Barton spent some years in Europe where she joined the International Red Cross. Later when she returned to the United States, she worked for the establishment of the American Red Cross and served as its first president until 1904, gradually becoming one of the world's best known women.

MARIE CURIE
(1867–1934)

Significance: Marie Curie became a very famous scientist who dedicated her entire life to science and to saving people's lives. There was much sadness in her life, and she became ill through the effects of working with radioactive elements, but her determination and hard work won her a place among the most important scientists who have ever lived.

Cancer is a disease that many people fear, but today there are a variety of treatments that are often very successful. One key treatment is radiation. One night in 1898, after many years of tedious work, Marie Curie discovered radium, the element used in radiation therapy. Thanks to her efforts and those of her husband Pierre Curie, the way was established for such an important treatment.

Marie Curie was born Maria Sklodowska on November 7, 1867, in Warsaw, Poland, and her nickname while growing up was Manya. She had an older brother, Jozef, and three older sisters: Sofia, Bronya and Helena. Poland at the time was under Russian control, and Poles with important jobs were forced out of work and replaced by Russians. Her parents, both teachers, lost their teaching posts and had to take in boarders to make ends meet. There was little time for moments of shared family affection, and a pat or quick hug from her parents was rare.

Maria was a small, timid child with long brown hair and delicate, hazel eyes, but behind her soft gaze was an exceptionally curious mind. She even taught herself to read before she went to school. Maria worked long hours helping with the meals, but she still managed to excel and even win a medal for excellence at the local high school. All her classes were taught in Russian, and the only history taught was Russian.

While she was still young, her sister Sofia and her mother contracted tuberculosis and died. It was a sad time, and she was frail and tired. At her father's insistence, she spent a year on a farm with relatives, which helped her to forget her sorrows and regain her strength.

Returning to Warsaw, Maria wished to pursue higher education, but there were no opportunities for women in Poland at that time, and to study abroad would take much money. Maria and her older sister Bronya worked out a plan to help each other. Bronya would go to Paris to study medicine and Maria would take a job as a governess and send the money she earned to Bronya. Later, Bronya would help Maria with her own education.

Before long Maria was teaching a class of eighteen children two extra hours a day in addition to her governess duties. At the same time she became passionately interested in science, particularly physics and mathematics, and she pored over books on these subjects at every possible moment.

When her sister qualified as a doctor, Maria went to join her in Paris. There was an additional reason that Maria, now taking the French name Marie, needed to get away from Poland. She had fallen in love with Kazimierz, the son of the house, but at this time she was merely a governess and not considered to be a suitable wife for the oldest son of such a wealthy family. Many years later, when Marie had become famous and a statue of her was erected in Warsaw, Kazimierz was known to gaze in thought at her likeness.

Still timid and shy, but now an attractive young woman, Marie was unsure about leaving Poland and her father, but finally she packed her bags, took one last look at Warsaw and headed to Paris and several years of poverty. Because she couldn't afford heat in winter, she kept warm by staying in bed and piling coats over her thin blankets. She entered the Sorbonne (University of Paris), where she studied physics and mathematics and graduated at the top of her class.

In 1894 she met French physicist Pierre Curie, and they were married the following year. Not caring what people thought, Marie refused to waste money on a white wedding dress; instead, she chose a plain dress that she could wear to work afterward. Bicycles had just become popular, so for their honeymoon, Marie and Pierre made a bicycle tour of France.

A period of hard work in research and teaching began when they returned from their bicycle honeymoon. A couple of years later their first child, Irene, was born. It was unusual at that time for women to return to work after having a baby, but Marie was determined to continue with her scientific research. When she left her daughter with a babysitter, some people thought she was neglecting her child. In fact she was a very loving mother and was very close to her two daughters all her life.

Drawn to the recent discoveries of X-rays and radiation from uranium salts, the Curies worked together on radioactivity. Marie decided that for her doctorate she would study uranium rays. With very little equipment and no money. Marie was to make an important scientific discovery that would save thousands of lives. First she discovered that the metallic element thorium also emits radiation. Then she found that the mineral pitchblende was more radioactive than either pure uranium or thorium, so it must contain another element that no one had yet discovered. Pierre and Marie decided to work together to find this new element, which they called radium.

It took years and many tons of pitchblende, which looks like ordinary dirt. Pitchblende contains only the tiniest amount of radium, and it was very difficult to extract. Marie had to stir huge pots of it for hours at a time. Then one day, as they opened their storage shed door, they saw in the darkness a faint blue glow. It was a tiny speck of pure radium! It had taken eight metric tons of pitchblende to produce one gram of radium.

We know today how dangerous radiation is, and for even very low level X-rays, at the dentist, for example, the technician is shielded from exposure. The Curies worked constantly with radioactive materials, and they suffered from strange pains in their limbs, excessive fatigue and lingering colds. Some photos of Marie during this time show a fragile, weary figure with wisps of unkempt hair falling loose, her thoughts clearly elsewhere. Three of the Curies' notebooks were considered too dangerous to handle because of radioactivity even 75 years after they had been written. Scientists have discovered, however, that handled properly, radiation can cure diseases such as cancer by being directed onto the unhealthy cells to destroy their growth.

The Curies became world famous, and they could have become very rich by patenting their discovery, but they chose to give their secret away to the public because they knew it would save many lives. In 1903 the Curies and another colleague were awarded the Nobel Prize in physics for their radioactivity research.

Marie became the first woman to hold a teaching post at the Sorbonne, but it happened as the result of a tragic accident in which her husband was run over and killed by a horse-drawn carriage. The university offered her Pierre's position as head of the physics department. Although Marie was deeply affected by her husband's death, she was determined to go on with their research, so she accepted the position. Very soon she demonstrated that her own work was worthy of world recognition, and in 1911 she was awarded the Nobel Prize in chemistry for her discovery of radium and another element, polonium.

During World War I Marie Curie decided to serve in the war in a way that was uniquely helpful. She oversaw the installation of X-ray equipment into ambulances, thus enabling doctors to know right away what was wrong so that they could act quickly and save lives. Marie hated the war that killed and injured so many young soldiers, but her hard work meant that in just one year, her team of helpers X-rayed over a million men.

By the late 1920s Marie's health began to deteriorate and she was slowly going blind. When she was 66 years old she became ill with a blood disease, today known as the cancer called leukemia, and she died on July 4, 1934.

JANUSZ KORCZAK
(1878–1942)
(A.K.A. HENRYK GOLDSZMIT)

Significance: The story of Janusz Korczak (pronounced *Kor-shack*) can be used to teach about the Third Reich and World War II.

Janusz Korczak was born into an assimilated Jewish family in Warsaw, Poland, at a time when the country was controlled by Russia. His mother's name was Cecylia Glebicki and his father's name was Jozef Goldszmit. Korczak's birth name was Henryk Goldszmit, and he later took the name of Janusz Korczak after using it as a writing pseudonym.

Physically he was small in build with intense but vulnerable eyes and a delicate face. As a dreamy child growing up in the city with few places to play, he escaped frequently into his imagination. It was bad manners to hang around the kitchen with the servants, but he did because the cook told stories. Family life was not a reliable source of stable comfort, primarily because his father was emotionally unpredictable, suffering a series of breakdowns.

An early theme in his life was discovering his Jewishness since his family was not at all connected to religious orthodoxy. In his earliest school years he was tutored by governesses, and then he attended Russian elementary schools where no Polish was allowed to be spoken. In that repressive atmosphere, he was strongly impressed by a prank that occurred; acting on a dare, a boy urinated on a blackboard eraser, was caught, and received a harsh spanking. That incident and other similar ones caused Henryk to become so nervous that his parents withdrew him from school. One lesson was branded into his mind: Children are not respected by adults.

His father's mental health worsened and he was institutionalized. The family's finances spiraled downward to the point that his mother began taking household valuables to the pawnshop to get money for daily expenses. Over the next few years the family was forced to abandon their spacious apartment. Korczak's father died in 1896, possibly a suicide. Henryk began tutoring to support his mother and sister and discovered that he liked children. He began writing, but it was too risky as a profession that would provide a stable income. Between being a medical student and writer, he led a tortured double life. He trained as a pediatrician, served as a military doctor, and then began practicing medicine in Warsaw.

Meanwhile his philosophy was developing: No cause, no war, was worth depriving children of their natural right to happiness. Korczak gained a reputation among his patients and circle of friends for his wealth of stories and magic tricks. His best medicine was his soothing presence and ability to take a sick child on his knee and tell a cheerful story. In 1910 he gave up his medical practice to run an orphanage. During this period he also had his own radio program. For vacations, he made yearly trips to Palestine and visited its kibbutzim.

September 1939: Warsaw was attacked by Germany. The Poles were waiting for France and Britain to rescue them. In spite of the danger, Korczak refused the urging of friends to send the children back to relatives and close the orphanage. During the air raids, the number swelled to 150 children. People didn't know if it would be better to flee to the Russian zone to the East. After three weeks of resistance, Warsaw fell to the Germans, and the German occupation began. At least there were soup kitchens and free bread.

Then a new terror began: Jews and Poles were rounded up for work details. Jewish schools and businesses were closed. Beginning on December 1, 1939, all Jews were required to wear the armband with the blue Star of David. Korczak, in quiet defiance, refused to wear one. In January 1940 he made his last diary entry for the next two years, turning all his energy into getting food and essentials for the orphans.

At first, hope was high that the Allies would defeat the Germans quickly, but then Nazis invaded Norway and the reality of Nazi power became evident as they continued to extend their occupation in all directions. In September 1940 on Yom Kippur, the Jewish ghetto in Warsaw was established. Korczak was forced to find a new building within the ghetto. His Gentile friends tried to convince him to go into hiding, but he was afraid of jeopardizing the safety of the children. The deadline for taking residency within the ghetto was November 30, setting off a moving frenzy of Poles and Jews; the move was orchestrated like a parade. During the hectic activity, Korczak was thrown in jail for a month when he complained about their cart of potatoes being taken. In spite of the outer chaos and uncertainty, Korczak was adamant that rhythm be maintained in the orphanage; lessons continued, including Hebrew. He wanted to give them hope above all else. Small concerts were arranged to raise money for support.

In December 1941 there was still a general feeling of hope. Germans had met resistance in Russia, and the Americans entered the war after the bombing of Pearl Harbor on December 7. But they did not know the first extermination camp had been set up. For Christmas/Hanukkah the orphanage put on a play and the children enjoyed gifts under a garbage truck.

By May 1942 the ghetto's size was decreased routinely. Frequently knocking on doors and shouts were heard in the night; shots were fired in the street. Korczak began his diary again; he knew death was near; his body was so fatigued and wasted. Daily life was becoming very difficult. On July 18, 1942, Korczak began work on a play with the children. Called "The Post Office," it was an escape, a fantasy—and dealt with death. The play centered on the inspirational figure of King Matt holding a flag, and the children played and imitated the character endlessly.

On July 22, 1942, came the evacuation of 6000 people to trains and resettlement in the East. Every deportee was allowed seven pounds of luggage including valuables and food for three days. Some were actually relieved to be getting out of the ghetto. Korczak's orphanage was spared this final time. The Polish Gestapo commander in charge took potassium cyanide rather than hand over helpless children.

On August 6, 1942, came the Last March. A Nazi soldier blew a whistle at the door of the orphanage: "Alle Juden raus!" They were given 15 minutes to collect their things. There were 4000 Jews from Warsaw in this final expulsion. They were going 60 miles northeast to Treblinka and gas chambers. With Korczak were 192 children and 10 adults. They took their flag of King Matt and began singing as they walked in rows of four, with dignity. Some soldiers saluted instinctively. Korczak boarded the trains with the children and was never heard from again.

MOHANDAS GANDHI
(1869–1948)

Significance: Gandhi was the father of three non-violent revolutions: 1) against colonialism, 2) against violence and 3) against racism.

Mohandas Gandhi was born on October 2, 1869, into a Hindu family of the merchant caste. The British Empire was at its peak and had ruled India for three centuries.

Gandhi was of slight build with very prominent ears. He was smaller and skinnier than most of the other boys, and he avoided lingering after school to prevent possible teasing about his size or his ears that stuck out. As a student Gandhi was only average, but he refused to cheat. At night he slept with the light on because he was afraid of ghosts in the dark. According to custom, he was married at age thirteen to Kasturbai, and their son was born when Gandhi was age nineteen.

Gandhi's father died and his older brother became the head of the household. Money was in short supply, and the family jewelry was sold to pay for his education.

To complete his education, Gandhi studied law in England for three years. Upon his return to India, he took a position as a lawyer but failed miserably in court because he was too shy, a situation that distressed his family greatly. He was soon offered an opportunity in South Africa.

While working in South Africa, he discovered that he was considered a member of an inferior race. Experiencing racism in such a virulent form caused him to become dedicated to the concept of non-violent resistance. His policy of passive resistance to authorities was based in part on the writings of Russian author Leo Tolstoy and American author Henry David Thoreau, as well as on the teachings of Jesus Christ. For twenty years Gandhi protested against discriminatory treatment, and he was jailed repeatedly. By law, Indians were among those second-class citizens required to carry a work permit or face deportation; whites were not required to carry similar passes. His greatest success came in 1914 when he and General Jan C. Smuts reached an agreement that lifted some of the harsh restrictions on Indians in South Africa.

In 1915 Gandhi fell ill and returned to India. He founded an ashram and strove to improve working conditions and break the caste system that kept the untouchables at the lowest rung of society. The kindness he showed to all living creatures caused him to be compared to Buddha. The foundation of his spiritual belief was that God represented "absolute truth."

During World War I he supported the British, hoping Britain would award self-rule to India after the war. When that didn't happen, he began fasting and leading non-violent protests such as work stoppages and boycotts of cotton cloth. Cotton was grown as an export crop in India at the time, shipped to the mills in Britain, and the cloth was then brought back and forced upon the Indian public. As a protest, spinning and weaving were revived throughout the country, and spinning in particular became a symbol of national unity. Gandhi himself dedicated some time each day to spinning. The image of his slender, brown body dressed only in a loincloth, and sitting before a simple spinning wheel, remains today a potent reminder of his determination and dedicated simplicity.

Gandhi could clearly see how damaging British economic control was to his country. Raw materials, such as cotton in particular, were shipped very cheaply to Great Britain where they were used in the manufacture of goods, woven textiles in the case of cotton. Then the woven textiles were sent back to India for sale, and Indians had little choice but to buy at inflated prices since the British had made it illegal to spin or weave in India. Meanwhile the self-sufficiency of the Indian people was being undermined as domestic skills, such as weaving, were not being practiced. Gandhi understood that the basic economy of India was in jeopardy, and he saw a similar danger for many other developing countries who were controlled by colonial powers.

Gandhi became the leader of the independence movement and the most powerful individual in all of India, but he lived the simple lifestyle of the country's most impoverished. British officials could do little to thwart him. In 1922 he was arrested and sentenced to six years in prison because he was considered a revolutionary. When imprisoned he fasted, and the authorities were forced to release him, knowing that the country would explode if Gandhi were to die in prison.

The British forced taxes on the Indian population as a way to pay for their government expenses. One tax law was particularly upsetting to Indians, and that was a tax on salt. Salt was a basic necessity, especially in the low coastal areas where the warm climate caused people to sweat so much and they needed salt to replenish what they lost through perspiration in the heat. The traditional salt beds had been confiscated and fenced off by the British government. In March 1930 Gandhi led a small band of followers toward the sea with the intention of gathering salt in protest of the British control. Along the way thousands more joined the march, and at the seashore Gandhi implored them to begin to make salt wherever was "most convenient and comfortable" for them. He began himself by picking up a lump of mud and salt (some say just a pinch, some say just a grain) and boiled it in seawater to make the commodity which no Indian could legally produce—

table salt. A pinch of salt from Gandhi himself sold for about $750 at the time. By the end of a month, the government had jailed over 60,000 people! On the night of May 4, Gandhi was sleeping on a cot under a mango tree. Shortly after midnight over thirty British soldiers arrived; one of them shone a torch in Gandhi's face to waken him and arrest him.

The effects of the salt march were felt across India, and thousands of people made salt or bought it illegally until the government finally relented. This protest became known as the Salt March of 1930, and although independence did not come for several more years, it represented a turning point in the struggle.

During World War II from 1939 to 1944, Gandhi refused to participate or give support to Britain. In the end, all the political clout and military might of the British government were overcome by a peaceful man in a loincloth. Finally, on August 15, 1947, India as a Hindu nation was granted independence, but Pakistan was separated as a Muslim nation. The following year, while still working for peace in a country torn by religious division, Gandhi was assassinated by a Hindu nationalist.

Gandhi was an inspiration to another follower of non-violence—Martin Luther King, Jr. Another of Gandhi's greatest admirers was Albert Einstein.

Speaking in 2001 Nelson Mandela had these words about Gandhi's critique of advanced industrial society: "He is not against science and technology, but he places priority on the right to work and opposes mechanization to the extent that it usurps this right. Large-scale machinery, he holds, concentrates wealth in the hands of one man who tyrannizes the rest. He favors the small machine; he seeks to keep the individual in control of his tools, to maintain an interdependent love relation between the two, as a cricketer with his bat or Krishna with his flute."

HELEN KELLER
(1880–1968)

Significance: Known for her humanitarian work for the treatment of the handicapped, Helen Keller's life is a profound story of one person's struggle to overcome adversity.

Imagine how determined a blind, deaf and dumb person would need to be to do something as complicated and demanding as attend college. The lectures would need to be repeated by an interpreter who could use sign language, books would need to be in Braille, and a special typewriter would be needed for her written papers. Over a hundred years ago such accommodations were nonexistent for handicapped persons.

In 1899, 19-year-old Helen Keller applied to Radcliffe College, the sister school to Harvard and well known for its high admissions standards. Radcliffe students came from the best high schools in the country, and Helen had never even attended a regular school. The dean of the college turned her application down, politely but firmly, explaining that she would be better off studying on her own. Helen was equally polite and firm, and she renewed her application to Radcliffe. While she was waiting for an answer, she received scholarship offers from two other excellent colleges, Cornell University and the University of Chicago, but she turned them down and remained stubbornly focused on Radcliffe. The next year Radcliffe admitted her, and her teacher Anne Sullivan spelled the lectures into her hand until she graduated four years later with honors. Such stubbornness made her early days a painful trial for everyone, Helen included, but her willfulness was transformed into positive directions by the amazing work of Anne Sullivan.

Helen was born on June 27, 1880, in a small Alabama town, the daughter of well-to-do parents, Arthur and Kate Keller. As a baby, she was lively, friendly, and, her parents insisted, unusually bright. When she was 19 months old, she became acutely ill with a mysteriously high fever, resulting in her becoming both deaf and blind within a few days In spite of the family's wealth and position in the community, there was nothing anyone could do to erase the tragedy. Lost in a world of silent darkness, Helen forgot what speech she had learned before her illness, and even the idea of language soon disappeared. With only a kind of primitive sign language to connect her to the family, her communication was reduced to cries of pain or need and grunts of pleasure. When she wanted her mother, she pulled her hair into a knot at the back of her head; for her father, she pretended to put on glasses. Her behavior was soon punctuated with violent outbursts of screaming and raging tantrums, and it seemed that no one could handle her or teach her anything, even though it was evident that she was very intelligent.

Her mischievous antics kept the family on high alert. Once, after she had discovered what keys were, she locked her mother in the pantry for three hours. Her mother kept pounding on the door while Helen sat on the steps and laughed with glee as she felt the pounding on the floorboards. Another time she found her baby sister sleeping in her doll's cradle and tried to dump her onto the floor. The Keller family's desperation increased along with their daughter's.

The Kellers took Helen to many specialists, all of whom had no hopeful advice to offer. One, however, suggested consulting the inventor Alexander Graham Bell, who was also a teacher of deaf people. Through his contacts, a teacher for Helen was found at the Perkins Institute for the Blind in Boston, Massachusetts. Anne Sullivan, a 21-year-old orphan of Irish immigrants, was chosen for the task. Arthur and Kate Keller were skeptical about Anne's youth and overall qualifications, but they were desperate. The association between Helen and Anne lasted until Anne's death in 1936.

Anne's first task was to break through the barrier of darkness and silence that enveloped Helen. The going was often rough. Early in the relationship she lost her two front teeth, knocked out by Helen in one of her fits of rage. Using a finger alphabet, Anne spelled onto the palm of Helen's hand the names of familiar things, such as "doll" and "cup." The first big breakthrough came when Anne pumped water from a well onto Helen's hand and spelled out the word "water." Helen suddenly realized that everything had its own name, and her capacity to learn was suddenly unleashed. She demanded to know the spelling, or finger symbols, for everything around her. By the end of that day, she had learned thirty new words, and within three months she knew three hundred words!

Two years later she was reading and writing fluently using the Braille system, which consists of arrangements of raised dots representing letters and combinations of letters. Because many dots are required for each word, Braille is a slow method of writing, but Helen took to it at once. When Helen was ten, she begged to learn to speak. At first this seemed impossible, but Anne discovered that Helen could learn sounds by placing her fingers on her teacher's larynx and feeling the vibrations. Helen's pronunciation always remained difficult to understand, but with Anne as an interpreter, she could convey her thoughts to others.

During her Radcliffe days, Helen received no special consideration for her handicaps. She earned excellent grades and so impressed her English professor that she was encouraged to write the story of her life for the *Ladies' Home Journal* magazine. Her autobiography,

The Story of My Life, was a great success; it is read today in fifty languages. The proceeds from the book were an important basis for financial independence, because the Keller family had fallen on hard financial circumstances. Through other essays and articles, Helen continued to explain the problems encountered by the deaf and blind. As one example of the possible but little known problems that plague the blind, Helen's eyes continued to cause her trouble, and for both medical and cosmetic reasons, they were removed and replaced with glass ones.

In 1913 Helen was persuaded that public speaking tours would make her mission of aiding the deaf and blind more effective. To help audiences understand her speech, Anne repeated Helen's words to the listeners. Helen also began to travel and lecture throughout the world, enlisting the aid of many famous people who were eager to meet her. While she was still only a young girl and her fame was beginning to spread, President Cleveland arranged to meet her, and after that, every president during her lifetime invited her to the White House. Mark Twain sang her praises and admired her writing. Philanthropist Andrew Carnegie often gave financial aid to public figures he admired, and he offered Helen an annual income. She accepted only after she became alarmed about Anne's failing health.

Carnegie's support enabled Helen and Anne to hire an assistant to help with their correspondence, finances, housekeeping and endless callers. Polly Thomson, a 24-year-old Scotswoman, became their secretary-housekeeper and remained with Helen for 45 years. When Anne Sullivan died in 1936 at age 70, Polly remained Helen's assistant until her own death.

Helen Keller's name was magic to the public. The warmth of her personality seemed to melt all hearts, from Henry Ford to John D. Rockefeller. She received many honors and awards, and she served on many commissions for the blind. She was also a staunch pacifist and active in social causes. After World War II (1939–1945), she visited wounded veterans in American hospitals and lectured in Europe on behalf of the physically disabled.

Helen died quietly on June 1, 1968, a few weeks before her 88th birthday. Through her writing, public speeches and example of dedicated service, she had a profound impact on the world's treatment and education of the handicapped.

Mao Zedong
(1893–1976)

Significance: The leader of the Chinese revolution and the Communist takeover of China, Mao was chairman of the Chinese People's Republic from 1949 to 1966.

A tremendous crowd of 100,000 supporters filled Tiananmen Square with their gaze focused on the balcony of the Gate of Heavenly Peace that overlooked the city of Beijing, and a hushed quiet spread rapidly as a tightly wrapped fabric bundle rose up in the air on the adjacent flagpole. A huge red flag with five yellow stars was unfurled as guns fired in salute. As Mao stepped up on the platform and stretched out his hands to proclaim the beginning of the Chinese People's Republic, the crowd roared and roared its delighted approval. That Mao was dressed in the simple gray tunic and trousers of a peasant was a point not lost on the people who cheered the new leader of China. After his speech, Mao watched the parade below that included the People's

Liberation Army, a string of army tanks and a stream of civilians shouting, "Long live Chairman Mao!" As the evening sky darkened, fireworks exploded throughout the sky. Dancers and musicians entertained the people with revolutionary songs.

The Chinese Communist Party had begun 28 years earlier with a small group of revolutionaries, and on October 1, 1949, Mao was acknowledged as the head of the most populous country on earth with over one-fifth of the world's population.

Mao was born on December 26, 1893, in central China in a mud-brick house with a thatched roof. The house stood beside a lotus pond at the foot of a wooded hill. As was the custom at birth, his mother, Wen Qimei, did not bathe him for three days, and at one month his hair was shaved except for a small tuft on top. According to traditional belief, this tuft of hair held the baby firmly to life. Mao's father, Mao Rensheng, was an uneducated but prospering rice farmer, and compared to others at that time, the family was fairly comfortable.

As a young child Mao had black hair, dark eyes, broad cheeks, a wide chin with a distinguishing mole and a twinkle in his eyes when he smiled. Later, as an adult, he was of medium height and stocky build.

Mao's mother took him to the Buddhist temple and taught him the principles of compassion and generosity, and although her husband was a religious skeptic and disapproved of giving charity, she gave rice to beggars during times of famine. Because his father wanted him to master the abacus and keep the family accounts, Mao was sent to the village school at the age of eight. He was also expected to memorize the texts of the great philosopher Confucius. Mao found adventure stories and tales of Chinese rebels more interesting.

Mao's father was harsh with him, and it turned out that the schoolmaster was equally so. Once Mao ran away from school to avoid yet another beating and, also afraid to return to his father's house, he wandered alone for three days. By the time he returned, the anger of the two men had subsided and they were relieved to find him alive and well. From that experience, Mao learned that active protest often leads to better treatment than meek submissiveness.

As Mao continued his work on the farm and studies on the side, he became aware of the problems in China. Poverty and famine were constant pressures on the peasant population. China was divided between the north controlled by warlords and the south which was under the control of the revolutionary Sun Yat-sen. From his studies, Mao learned about China's great history and how the Chinese regarded their country as the center of the world and the only true civilization. They were proud of their many contributions to the world, including the art of papermaking, tea, gunpowder, printing and the compass. He learned about the Qin, Han and Qing dynasties; the building of the Great Wall; and exploitation from Great Britain and Japan during the 1800s. During these student years, Mao's own revolutionary philosophy was formed, steeped in sympathy for Chinese peasant life.

One example of Mao's rebellious nature is seen in his refusal to wear his hair the way the ruling Manchu government demanded. All men were forced to wear their hair in one long braid, a queue, which hung down the middle of the back. As a sign of disobedience, Mao cut off his queue and convinced some of his classmates to follow suit. When some refused, Mao and a comrade attacked them and cut their hair.

After finishing his schooling, Mao became a teacher and librarian, all the while looking for ways to improve the lives of the Chinese people. In 1921 he and a small group of like-minded young people founded the Chinese Communist Party. They decided to join efforts with the revolutionary Sun Yat-sen and later Chiang Kai-shek.

Over the next few years they adopted the ideas of Lenin who had successfully led a revolution in Russia. There was a lot of discussion about where their efforts should be concentrated, and it was decided that the countryside was the place to create a revolutionary elite since ninety percent of the population consisted of poor peasants. Mao won the respect of the peasants by driving away landlords and giving them their own land to farm.

A split developed between Chiang Kai-shek who held top power as leader of the Nationalist People's Party (Kuomintang) and Mao who led the Communists. Chiang Kai-shek purged the communists from his party, and Mao led his "Red Army," as his communist guerrilla forces were called, on a march to establish a new stronghold in the northwestern mountainous area of China.

Mao's pregnant wife, He Zizhen, was among the supporters on the year-long trek. Their two-year-old son was left behind with Mao's brother, and they never saw the child again. The marchers, covering about twenty miles a day, endured terrible hardships. He Zizhen tried to do nice things for her husband during the rest periods, but he scarcely noticed because his mind was always occupied. He Zizhen gave birth to two more children during the march, a boy who lived only briefly and a girl who was left with a peasant woman for safekeeping. Once He Zizhen was seriously wounded when she used her body to shield a soldier from gunfire, and she suffered a terrible blow to her head. She was unconscious for days and had to be carried on a stretcher as the march continued.

The Long March, as it was later called, was 6000 miles long, and it is estimated that about 30,000 survived out of the 100,000 who began. The greatest accomplishment was that Mao became well-known and popular among the people of the countryside.

During the Japanese invasion of China in World War II, Chiang Kai-shek collaborated with Mao Zedong and the Red Army to defeat the Japanese army. As soon as the war ended, however, the Red Army began a war against the Nationalists led by Chiang Kai-shek, and on October 1, 1949, a victorious Mao announced the establishment of the People's Republic of China, ending the rule of the Nationalists.

In 1958 Mao announced the Great Leap Forward which was a radical reorganization of China's social structure intended to increase agricultural and industrial production. People were forced to live on huge communes where each family worked and received a small share of the profits. The people lived in dormitories, sharing daily affairs and organizing their work in groups. The massive experiment was a failure and the country returned to a more traditional economy whereby people could at least keep small private gardens for themselves.

In 1966 Mao initiated the Cultural Revolution in which full blame for China's economic failures was focused on the privileged class, especially intellectuals and families of wealth. Students and young workers joined the Red Guard and were trained to spy on and capture enemies of the revolution. During this period it was commonplace for people to be forced to publicly condemn even their own family members.

The government launched a campaign against enemies and ideas threatening to the state called the Four Olds: old ideas, habits, customs and cultures. People were not allowed to criticize the government, and all art, music and writing had to appear patriotic. Frequently citizens who ran afoul of the Party line were sent to prison or labor camps for reeducation; hundreds of thousands simply disappeared.

The Communist Party considered religion a threat to the authority of the government, and they expected that religion would fade away as the people were educated according to party-endorsed scientific viewpoints. All public religious festivals were forbidden. Officially all religions ended, but many went underground, primarily Buddhism and Taoism, but also Christianity.

Overall under Mao, the status of women was improved. Traditional Chinese culture was centered entirely on the lives of the men, so much so that in ancient China girls did not have names until they married. After marriage, the bride joined her husband's family and became a virtual servant to her mother-in-law. Under Mao's rule, child marriages were outlawed and women ceased to be such second class citizens. He famously liked to say that women hold up half the sky. Still, families preferred sons who carried on the family name and held the more important jobs and positions.

Swimming was an unlikely but important theme in Mao's life. As a youngster he liked to write poems, and one of his earliest celebrated the excitement of swimming fast enough to beat a breaking wave. He considered swimming a way to strengthen the body and calm the mind. When he was in his 60s and at the height of his political power, swimming became an important escape from the rigors of his demanding life. For his personal use a large pool was constructed inside his heavily guarded compound. He loved to swim alone in the rough ocean waters off the north China coast where the Communist Party leadership met for its annual meetings. Although his personal physician begged him not to, he also swam in the polluted river near his compound, undisturbed by the globs of human excrement floating alongside. He enjoyed floating for miles downstream on his back with his stomach in the air, head relaxed and arms and legs scarcely moving. His security guards were afraid that he would sink, but he was unperturbed.

Mao was unsinkable in political life as well. He had many enemies: party rivals, landlords, Chiang Kai-shek, the Japanese, the Soviet Union and the United States. On the positive side he saved China from foreign oppression, gave land to struggling peasants, improved education for all and raised the social position of women. On the negative side, his policies led to economic disaster, starvation and violence. Recently discovered facts have come forward indicating that once Mao achieved power, he was corrupted by it and the Chinese people suffered as a result. No matter how one looks at his life, he left an indelible mark on China's modern history.

After suffering his third heart attack, Mao died on September 9, 1976. The Chinese people wore black armbands and decorated everywhere with white paper flowers to show their genuine grief. In just the few years that followed, the government ushered in a new era of openness to the world that has led to the rapidly growing economy of today.

NIEN CHENG
(1915–2009)

Significance: Nien Cheng witnessed the Cultural Revolution and the beginning of communism in China. Her autobiography, *Life and Death in Shanghai*, chronicles the changes brought on by the revolution.

"Open the gate! Open the gate! Are you all dead? Why don't you open the gate?" According to Nien Cheng's autobiography, these were the shouts of the Red Guard as they pounded on her gate and honked their truck horn. These young people had been organized by the Communist Party to raid the homes of the wealthy. Nien Cheng tried to appear composed as she came downstairs. The group of thirty or so Red Guard youths announced themselves: "We are the Red Guards. We have come to take revolutionary action against you!"

Nien Cheng had prepared herself and responded, a copy of the constitution in her hand, "It's against the

Constitution of the People's Republic of China to enter a private house without a search warrant." One of the Guard members seized the document from her and tossed it on the floor. He told her that the constitution had been abolished and that the teachings of Chairman Mao were the basis of their authority.

Another comrade shook her fist under Nien Cheng's nose, spat on the floor and threatened her to bow her head in submission or suffer the consequences. Another member pulled a large mirror off the wall and smashed it. They locked her in the dining room while they searched the house. Nien Cheng's only daughter was away that evening for work at a film studio.

Her husband had died some years earlier of cancer, and Nien Cheng was employed by Shell Oil Company, where her husband had held an important position. Nien Cheng had been careful not to flaunt her high standard of living, which included three servants, or to show off her collection of Chinese antiques. But this forced entry by the Red Guard was the beginning of seven years of imprisonment and harassment.

Nien Cheng said goodbye to antique plates, vases and figures as she heard them being smashed in the rooms upstairs. Later she witnessed one of the young Guards crushing a delicate porcelain cup with his foot, enjoying her pained reaction. Impulsively, she leaped forward to stop him from crushing a second cup, but he kicked her away, accusing her of trying to protect her possessions. She tried to argue that the cups were hundreds of years old and part of their cultural heritage, but the Guards rejected her argument, saying, "The purpose of the Great Proletarian Revolution is to destroy the old culture!" The destruction continued. Fur coats and dresses were cut up, food was strewn about, furniture was tossed around and her books were burned in a bonfire on the lawn. She was allowed to pack one suitcase for herself, and her life was forever changed.

Nien was born in Beijing in 1915 into a very traditional family. Her parents' marriage had been arranged. She was the eldest of seven children, three other girls and three boys. All were well educated, and some even had studied abroad. Two sisters went to the United States, married there and became American citizens. Nien attended a girls' boarding school where she excelled, becoming student body president, working on the school newspaper and playing basketball. Later she studied at Beijing University and then attended the London School of Economics, majoring in economics. Her type of education emphasized memorization, and she acquired a superior memory; the disadvantage was that her education did not encourage creative thinking. Nien herself, reflecting in later years, felt that a blend of the two forms would result in a better education.

Nien met her husband Kang-chi Cheng in London, and in 1940 after World War II began, they returned to China where he became a diplomatic officer for the ruling Kuomintang (National People's Party) government. Life was not easy during this period of war with Japan. When the Japanese bombed their city, they retreated to a bomb shelter under their house. Some people used deep caves in the mountainsides for shelter. In the summer of 1941, a bomb landed in front of their house, tearing off the roof and destroying some of the house. Nien was able to dig out clothing and suitcases, and soon after they were posted in the diplomatic service to Australia where they enjoyed happier days. Their daughter Meiping was born in Sydney, and memories include watching their toddler daughter play in the sand at the beach.

After the war Nien Cheng and Kang-chi returned to China under the idealistic hope that the Communists would unite the country and improve the standard of living for the people. They did not foresee the class struggle that was coming nor did they know the risk for the educated class.

With the permission of the Communist Party, Kang-chi became the general manager of the Shanghai branch of Shell International Petroleum Company. The Chengs led a glamorous life with plenty of entertaining and socializing. They were able to travel abroad several times. Then in 1957 Kang-chi died of cancer, widowing Nien Cheng at age 42. Until the time of her arrest, she worked as a special advisor at Shell, but harassment sessions by the Communists began within the company.

After Nien's arrest for being a capitalist enemy of the government, she spent six years in confinement, either under house arrest, in a prison cell, or in a hospital. When she was first sent to a detention house, she was told to undress. Her clothes were searched and then returned to her—except for her bra, because it was considered a bad form of Western dress. After that she was known only as No. 1806.

Meiping was not permitted to see her mother, but when Nien Cheng was allowed to go outside for exercise, she would occasionally find crumpled notes from Meiping in the bushes. Although these were often nearly disintegrated from the rain, they were a great boost to Nien Cheng's morale. Children of wealthy "capitalist" families were regularly harassed and forced to write confessions and self-criticisms. Meiping had to write self-criticisms because of her family background, and she was pressured to denounce her mother as a spy.

During the period of detention, Nien Cheng was repeatedly interrogated, beaten and tortured, but in spite of injuries and illnesses, she refused to make a confession. The worst torture she endured was being forced to wear extra-tight handcuffs for several days in a tiny cell until her wrists were oozing pus and blood, and she finally collapsed into unconsciousness.

Nien Cheng was never informed of outside events, so she was surprised when six and a half years after she had been brought to the detention house, she was suddenly told to pack up her things and leave. The authorities said that no charges would be filed against her because she was politically backward and ignorant and because she had shown some improvement in her thinking. Her goddaughter was waiting to take her home in a taxi. Hearing of her daughter's death, reportedly a suicide, was a tragic shock.

Political relations between China and the United States improved, and President Nixon made an historic trip to China, which influenced Mao Zedong to change some of his policies. In 1978, two years after Mao's death, Nien Cheng began seriously to consider leaving China for the U.S. After diplomatic relations had been reestablished between the two countries, she wrote to her sisters in the U.S. asking to be sent an invitation to visit for a "family reunion." Two years later she obtained her visa. She was allowed only one suitcase and one carry-on bag, and the only money she could take was worth twenty dollars. It was a shattering moment to leave the country of her birth.

Nien Cheng became a resident of Washington, D.C., and learned the ways of modern Westernized life. She wrote her autobiography and was called upon by the media when there were newsworthy events occurring in China. When the Chinese students flocked into Tiananmen Square in 1989 to call for greater democracy, many were killed by the Chinese army. During this crisis, Nien Cheng was asked for her expert analysis of the situation. Although readers of her book understandably view her as a woman of extraordinary courage, she considered that she only did what she believed was right.

Nien Cheng died on November 2, 2009, at the age of 94.

JOMO KENYATTA
(1893–1978)

Significance: Jomo Kenyatta was a major African revolutionary figure, leading Kenya in its successful fight against British colonial rule, which ended in 1963.

Growing up as a member of the Kikuyu tribe in the rich farming area of central Kenya, Kamau (Jomo Kenyatta) had a difficult childhood. He loved stories and enjoyed playing with friends. When his father died of a sudden illness, his mother Wambui went to be the second wife of his uncle, according to accepted custom. She gave birth to another son, a half brother, Ngengi.

The uncle was cruel, and Wambui returned to her own parents' home with the two children. "We are going to a place where there is plenty to eat," she said. There they were happy for a time. Then Kamau heard wailing and crying—his mother had died.

Kamau and his four-year-old brother were no longer welcome. He became the provider and decision maker, and they had little choice but to return to the village of their father and uncle. He was given a hut but he had to work hard, taking care of animals and helping other boys and men to hunt and build. He had to do "woman's work" such as sweeping, cooking, fetching water and collecting firewood. Kamau grew into a strong, tall teenager, doing all the work of both a mother and a father. With broad shoulders, excellent coordination and a handsome face, he possessed an air of confidence. People liked him; he joked a lot and was a good storyteller. He started wearing a brightly colored beaded belt called a *kinyata*.

To become independent of his father's family home, he moved to a distant village called Muthiga to join his grandfather, Jungu wa Magana, who was a witch doctor and wise seer who had his own kind of healing magic. His grandfather used a gourd filled with shells, stones and bones. He had extensive knowledge of herbal mixtures and could cure many illnesses.

His grandfather told Kamau stories of old, of the prophecy of the coming of the light-skinned people dressed like butterflies, carrying killing sticks and bringing great wealth. They will bring a huge snake with many legs, he predicted—an imaginative picture of the railroad.

Then one day a pale-faced stranger came to the village and Kamau discovered about reading and writing as another kind of "magic." In 1909 he entered the mission school, but he had to leave his machete at the door. He learned to read and write English, and also Swahili. Some teachers were very good people but some taught them to hate African traditions, which resulted in the boys' loss of confidence and sense of belonging to African society. At the mission school he and the other boys were forced to learn carpentry and make tables and chairs rather than pursue more advanced academic studies, which caused them to mutter among themselves that the whites just wanted them to be their servants. Kamau learned that Kenya was ruled by these British, and he came to understand the term "colonialism." He stayed at the school long enough to get the education he desired, and then he returned home.

There followed a few happy years during which he married Grace Wahu and started a family. Then terrible events began when the British government started taking land from Kenyans and giving it to British settlers and any other white people. Land is very important in African culture because contact with the soil is part of traditional worship. Land was also the source of livelihood. With no land to farm, many of the people were forced into menial jobs with the whites.

Kamau was lucky. He began in Nairobi in a civil service job as a meter reader, and then he was promoted to inspector at Nairobi Water Works. During the 1920s he changed his name to Kenyatta. He was a striking man, tall and towering with a rugged, bearded face and intense, intelligent eyes. Dressing smartly and often wearing brown boots and an American cowboy hat, he was an imposing figure. A charming and persuasive individual, he attended social events and frequented the horse races, thus meeting many influential people.

Resistance groups were forming during this period, and Kenyatta became actively involved. He joined the Kikuyu Central Association and was chosen to go to London as their representative. There he was surprised by gray skies, tall buildings, many cars and unfriendly people who did not greet each other in the street. In London he met other Africans fighting for independence. Kenyatta wanted to explain the African culture to Europeans, which led him to write his famous book, *Facing Mt. Kenya*, in 1938 while he was studying anthropology at the university. It demonstrated a strong African culture and undermined the European concept of Africans as savages.

While he was still in London, World War II began and he was unable to return to Kenya until the war ended. It was during this period that he remarried. In 1945 he returned to Kenya as a hero, quickly becoming a national leader. Able to address the people in both Swahili and Kikuyu, Kenyatta was a hypnotic speaker: Didn't we go to fight in their war? Yes! Didn't they tell us we would get our land back? Yes!! Have they given it back? No!!!

In 1947 India became independent of British colonial rule, and Kenyans were encouraged that they would soon gain similar independence. Kenyans had fought in the British army during World War II, and they returned to Kenya smart, angry and knowledgeable about guns. They began to organize themselves. They engaged in guerrilla warfare, especially in the area near Mt. Kenya, and came to be known as the Mau Mau. Because the British had a strong military force, the Mau Mau used surprise tactics and attacked police stations and farms of British settlers. Women risked their lives carrying food, guns and medicine to the warriors in the forest.

By 1952 fighting had intensified. Mau Mau homes were burned, people were murdered and crops were destroyed. Thousands of Mau Mau sympathizers were rounded up and held in outdoor prisons. Kenyatta avoided identification with the Mau Mau, but he was arrested nevertheless. His trial was in a remote northern town near Lake Turkana, and he was sentenced to seven years of hard labor.

Although he was very isolated, he was able to get books and managed occasional outside contact. To Kenyan people his name became magical: *Uhuru na Kenyatta!* Independence with Kenyatta!

The British control of the country was weakening, and as the Kenyans caused so much trouble with strikes, the British government had to give in to the demands of the people. In 1961 Kenyatta was freed; he was 70 years old.

Independence was negotiated in two steps. First there would be internal self-government beginning in 1963 with Kenyatta as Prime Minister. The spirit of "harambee"—pulling together—was the watchword of the people. Total independence and a constitution would follow as a second step, with Kenyatta as the first president. The matter of land distribution remained a question to resolve, and Kenyatta allowed the white farmers to stay if they wished. December 12, 1963, was Uhuru Day (Independence Day), and the black, red, green and white flag of Kenya was raised.

On August 21, 1978, Kenyatta died peacefully in his sleep with Mama Ngina at his side. People were allowed three days' leave from work for his funeral, and he was buried in a monument in Nairobi. Vice President Moi took over as head of the government.

NELSON MANDELA
(1918–2013)

Significance: Leader in the anti-apartheid movement and the first non-white to serve as president of South Africa, Mandela is one of the most recognized and respected international figures of the late 20th century.

Nelson Mandela is so well known that he has even reached comic book status. He has become a legend in his own lifetime. As a retired senior statesman in South Africa, he was forced to deal with his popularity in almost unimaginable ways. His legal representatives have had to go to court to prevent his name and image from being used by coin makers, food vendors, vineyards and even auto body shops. A person who wanted to use Mandela's famous prison number "46664" in his business telephone number was stopped. Mandela took great care not to allow his name to be used for commercial purposes, even rejecting the lecture circuit which is worth millions of dollars.

The respect he commanded was well deserved. He brought his country from the brink of a violent disaster to a place of hope. Even two decades ago, when he was released from his years in prison, he was already an international symbol and hero. There is a Mandela-endorsed HIV-AIDS organization that sells black teeshirts with the 46664 number, and Bono and Bill Clinton have been seen wearing them. Everyone has critics, even Nelson Mandela, but the dominant sentiments are affection and pride.

His story began on July 18, 1918, in a tiny village named Mvezo. His full name was Rolihlahla, which is Xhosa for "troublemaker," but his nickname was Buti. His father of the Mandiba clan was the proud chief of the village as were his father and grandfather before him. Mandela's father had four wives and thirteen children, and Mandela was the youngest son. They lived in a beautiful area of rolling hills where they kept cattle and grew crops.

White people ruled the area and had power over the local tribes. One day there was a dispute over the ownership of a cow that had wandered away from its owner. The cow was claimed and eaten by a neighbor, and Chief Hendry, Mandela's father, was called to straighten out the matter. The owner of the cow was not satisfied with the payment ordered by Chief Hendry and took his complaint to the local English magistrate. The magistrate instructed the chief to appear in court to testify, but Chief Hendry was a proud man and defied the order.

Because of his refusal, the English magistrate stripped Hendry of his chieftainship and his cattle, which were his source of wealth. Mandela, his mother and his sisters had to move to another village, and his father visited them when he could. In a nearby field his mother grew crops to feed her children, doing all the planting, weeding and harvesting. His sisters ground the maize, known as mealie meal, and cooked the sorghum, beans and pumpkin for supper. Mandela herded sheep and cattle by the time he was five years old.

At the suggestion of friends, Hendry decided to send his smart young son to school at age seven. Until that time, Mandela's only clothing had been a blanket worn over one shoulder and fastened at the waist. His father decided his son needed to wear English clothing for school, so he shortened the legs of a pair of his own trousers and tied them with a string at Mandela's waist. Feeling dressed like a king, Mandela began school, the first one in his family ever to attend. The English teacher gave him the name of Nelson on the first day.

Two years later Mandela's life changed completely with the death of his father from a lung disease. He loved his mother dearly, but his father was his hero. He resembled his father both in his looks, with high cheekbones and narrow eyes, and in his stubborn temperament. From his father he had learned the lesson of standing firm for what he believed was fair and just.

Because his mother could no longer afford to keep him in school, Nelson went to live with a wealthy and powerful relative, Chief Jongintaba, king of the Thembu people. The first time Mandela saw the chief was an impressive moment in the young boy's life: Chief Jongintaba drove up in an enormous car! Mandela lived with the chief's family for several years, and Jongintaba treated him as his son. Mandela attended the missionary school and learned more about Western ways. He also absorbed the stories of the Zulu and Xhosa kingdoms as he listened with enthusiasm to the ancient tales told by the village storyteller in the smoky firelight of evening. Being around Chief Jongintaba and the elders, Mandela witnessed a process of tribal decision-making that influenced his own style of leadership later on.

When he was sixteen, Mandela took part in a traditional Xhosa initiation into manhood. The ritual of circumcision is required for a Xhosa man to marry, inherit land or livestock, or participate in tribal ceremonies. The group of boys undergoing initiation began by building themselves grass huts along the river bank. On the eve of the ceremony, there was singing and dancing by the villagers until late. Then at early dawn, the boys bathed themselves in the river before lining up before the chief and elders. Exhibiting great bravery, each young man had his foreskin cut off by an *ingcibi*, or circumcision expert, as the elders looked on. They were instructed to bury their foreskins to represent the end of childhood and entry into manhood. Afterward, each young man was daubed all over with white clay, and they slipped into the huts for a period of days while they healed. After some days the ritual ended, first with a bath in the river, and then with music, speeches and gifts to each of the young men.

The chief sent Mandela to the best African schools in South Africa. There he met not only Thembu people from other areas for the first time, but he was surprised when he encountered a few white people who were open and friendly. He began to consider himself an African rather than identifying only with his tribal affiliation. Mandela was a popular and successful student; however, he ran into trouble when he protested to the authorities about what he considered unfair treatment and ended up being expelled.

Mandela returned to his village where Chief Jongintaba was furious with his behavior. Mandela agreed to make amends and return to school, but before he departed the chief called Mandela and his own son, named Justice, to tell them that he had arranged marriages for them—immediately! Even though arranged marriages were normal tribal procedure, the young men were in a rebellious state and chose to run away to Johannesburg instead. It was not easy to travel, and finally a friend arranged for them to catch a ride with a white woman. Because they were black, they had to ride in the back of the car.

In Johannesburg Mandela struggled to find a job and a place to live and ended up with a distant cousin. It was his extremely good fortune to get a job as a clerk with a white law firm that did some business with black clients. They liked him and allowed him to study law free of charge in his spare time. His weekly salary as an apprentice lawyer barely covered essentials, and like many other people, he walked to and from work to save money, six miles each way in his case. Seeing that he didn't have a suit to wear for work, one of the lawyers gave him an old one that Mandela wore for five years, patching it over and over. There were patches on the patches!

During his early lawyer years, Mandela made many friends who were politically active. Black Africans were being treated badly, and protest movements were simmering. Blacks were forced to live in reserved areas that lacked clean water and sanitation. They had to carry "pass books" everywhere they went to prove where they lived and where they worked. There were extra taxes frequently levied on the black population for civic improvements which they never saw. Buses were segregated, and the "African only" buses came much less often and were packed. Black people always went around to the back door.

The discrimination Mandela witnessed was beyond his endurance, and he joined the African National Congress (ANC), which campaigned on behalf of the rights of all Africans. He became one of their leaders and was involved in planning strikes and protest marches.

Then in 1948 the system of apartheid began which officially separated the black and white populations with strict laws and regulations. The laws became even more severe against blacks, and many were forced to resettle in so-called tribal homelands under dreadful conditions and where they had no family, jobs, or land of their own.

In 1945 Mandela married Evelyn Mase, a nurse, and they had two sons Thembi and Makgatho, and a daughter, Makaziwe. Family life did not mix easily with the danger and uncertainly of political activism. The marriage did not endure the strains of different political views, and they divorced. Mandela married again in 1958 to Winnie Madikizela, a social worker who shared his commitment to the struggle. In time they had two daughters.

Mandela was imprisoned numerous times over the years. He stayed on the move, using disguises and traveling at night from one safe house to another. Finally, in 1963, he was charged with attempting to overthrow the government of South Africa. He was facing a guilty verdict for treason, and the only serious question was the sentence: Would he face life imprisonment or the death penalty? Thoughts of his father's example of standing firm for one's belief must have been what supported him through the ordeal. He used the witness stand to make an international appeal against apartheid. Reporters from around the world were in attendance, and he spoke for four hours.

Mandela spent 27 years in prison on Robben Island, just off the coast from Cape Town, South Africa. Amazingly, his presence continued to be felt all across South Africa and even reached to other parts of the world. In the 1970s the slogans "Free Mandela" and "End Apartheid" could be seen on bumper stickers and freeway overpasses wherever there were sympathizers. In 1968 his oldest son Thembi was killed in a car crash but Mandela was not allowed to attend the funeral. In 1975 he began to write his memoirs so that the world would know the anti-apartheid story, and a prisoner being released smuggled out his writings.

Pressures intensified during the 1980s, both from within South Africa and from the international community, finally bringing Mandela's release on February 11, 1990. He helped author a new constitution for South Africa and became the president in the first election in which all Africans could vote. The lines stretched for blocks and the voting lasted for four days before all the ballots were cast. People waited patiently. Some faulted him that he made too many concessions to the South African whites who continued to own most of the land and wealth of the country. Many others praised him that such a change could be realized without massive bloodshed.

Mandela retired in 1999 at age 81. He married again, a woman named Graca Machel, and they went to live in Qunu, the village of his childhood. Even during retirement, he continued to meet with world leaders and further the cause of peace on the African continent. Mandela died on December 5, 2013, at his home in Johannesburg.

MARTIN LUTHER KING, JR.
(1929–1968)

Significance: Martin Luther King, Jr., was a leader of the Civil Rights Movement in the 1950s and 1960s in the Southern states. Slaves had been freed in 1865 at the end of the American Civil War, yet a century later segregation laws continued unfair treatment.

Martin Luther King, Jr., was born on January 15, 1929, in Atlanta, Georgia. In his short life of 39 years, he made such an impact on American society that his birthday is a national holiday. Martin's mother, Alberta, was a teacher, and his father, Martin Luther King, Sr., was a Baptist minister. His parents were well educated and devoutly religious. He had an older sister Christine and a younger brother Alfred.

Martin grew up in very different times than ours. Black people were not given a chance to have the same opportunities as white people. White people pushed blacks aside, taking the best houses, schools and jobs for themselves. When Martin was a young boy he didn't see these things yet. For example, he had two white boys as playmates.

He grew up in the church community, and he saw his parents working to gain equal treatment for black people. He attended schools with only black children. He liked music and singing, loved to read books and was always quiet in class. He liked arithmetic best, especially fractions. Martin learned fast and helped the slower children by encouraging them and giving them compliments. He loved drama and cherished the time he was chosen to recite Abraham Lincoln's Gettysburg Address and also Patrick Henry's "Give Me Liberty" speech. Obviously he was destined to be a fine orator.

He was peace-loving and mild-mannered in his actions but he became forceful in his speeches. He disapproved of violence. Once he was forced into a fight with a fellow student—a very painful experience for him, both because he was badly beaten by a bigger bully and also because he hated physical violence.

King believed in family, church, school and hard work. He studied hard and followed the rules of his parents and teachers. But as he grew older, he was troubled when he saw injustice, especially mistreatment of black people. In college, where he earned a doctorate degree in philosophy, he was exposed to the ideas of non-violent protest, ideas from people like Gandhi and Henry David Thoreau; they refused to obey unjust laws and were willing to be punished for breaking laws—

but they refused to resort to violence. Their method was called passive resistance.

King became a leader in the Civil Rights Movement. One of his biggest projects was the bus boycott in Montgomery, Alabama. Black people were protesting in a non-violent way by refusing to ride the buses. So many people from all over the country, both white and black, became interested in helping the blacks gain proper jobs, housing and voting rights that a huge rally was held in Washington, D.C., in 1963. Over 200,000 people attended, and the highlight was King's speech, "I have a dream…."

In 1964 King was awarded the Nobel Peace Prize. On April 3, 1968, he was assassinated in Memphis, Tennessee, by James Earl Ray. Rallies and candlelit ceremonies were held all over the country in his honor. We remember Martin Luther King, Jr., as a true revolutionary—a leader of the non-violent means of protest.

Some black people today still do not always get the fair treatment they deserve; the work of Martin Luther King is not finished. His life continues to serve as an inspiration for everyone today as we all strive to treat each other as brothers and sisters, and as we look for peaceful ways to settle our differences.

CÉSAR CHÁVEZ
(1927–1993)

Significance: Mexican American labor leader and co-founder of the United Farm Workers labor union, Chávez fought to improve the working and living conditions of migrant farm workers.

Born on March 31, 1927, César Estrada Chávez grew up with his five siblings on his family's farm near Yuma, Arizona. César's grandfather, Césario, was a poor farmer in Mexico who had come north looking for a better life in the United States. He obtained a farm in the 1880s by homesteading, and the land was inherited by Librado Chávez, César's father. Cotton was the main crop, but they also had small plots of watermelon, corn, squash and chilies. Chickens roamed in the shade of their adobe house, providing eggs and an occasional stew.

In 1937, when César was ten years old, a drought caused crop failures and César's father could not pay his bills. He was swindled by dishonest Anglos who talked him into a tax agreement and then broke the agreement, leaving the family with only their car and a few belongings. They loaded up their car and joined the great mass of nearly a million people in search of work in California and neighboring states. Farm work was all that they knew how to do, so they became migrant farm workers, with even the children picking cherries, plums, apricots, peaches and tomatoes from farm to farm in California. Workers were paid for each box they filled, and it was difficult to work fast enough to make more than a few cents each day. Many hours each day were often spent bending over to hoe weeds from around the crops in the fields. In some places there were work camps where they could stay, but at other times they had to sleep in their car. Sanitary conditions were miserable.

During the years of the Great Depression, the whole country was suffering with many people out of work and hungry. It was during this time when César and his brother Richard got their first paying job hunting gophers for local farmers. The gophers not only harmed crops, but they ruined the irrigation canals by digging tunnels that weakened them until they collapsed. The boys were paid one penny for each dead gopher, and they had to prove their claim by showing the tail of each gopher they killed. Other jobs they found included cracking walnuts, collecting bottles and chopping wood for neighbors. Once they had a job sweeping up spilled popcorn in a movie house, and it gave them a chance to see the Lone Ranger movies for free.

César did not like school as a child, probably because his English was so poor. The teachers were nearly all English-speaking Anglos, and Spanish was forbidden in school. He spoke Spanish outside of the classroom, and he remembers being punished with a ruler whacked on his knuckles for breaking the rule. Once his shoes gave out in the dead of winter, and he was filled with humiliation to come to school barefoot. He remembers having to endure racist comments, and he recalls seeing signs that read "whites only."

Because they were moving so often to follow the crops, César attended 37 schools in all. He left school after the eighth grade to be a full-time farm worker. His father had injured himself, and César did not want his mother, Juana, to work in the fields.

Although his school education was not a happy experience, education was his passion later in life, and he lined his office with hundreds of books on every subject. He was especially interested in the biographies of Gandhi and the Kennedys, and their lives served as examples to him for serving others. The life of St. Francis also made a strong impression on him.

César saw the field conditions as he was growing up, and he wanted to help migrant farm workers obtain better conditions and basic rights such as many unions had established for their members. In 1945 he went into the Navy; three years later he was back to work in the fields. In 1948 he married Helen Fabela, and they honeymooned in California by visiting all the California missions from Sonoma to San Diego. A couple of weeks later they were on their knees, cutting grapes. Later they worked together in the cotton fields. They settled in Delano, an agricultural town in the Central Valley, and together they had eight children.

In 1952 Chávez met Fred Ross who worked for the Community Service Organization (CSO), a Latino civil rights group. Chávez was able to get the workers together, and Ross was able to show them how to vote and fight for their rights. In 1958 Chávez became head of the CSO. During this period he became concerned about the competition for field work that was growing between Mexican Americans who were U.S. citizens and Mexican immigrants who came for temporary work. These Mexican workers, known as *braceros*, worked for lower wages, and the owners squeezed everything they could out of them. Chávez could see clearly how one group of poor people was being pitted against another, more desperate group.

In 1962 Chávez joined forces with Dolores Huerta and together they started a union just for migrant workers, the National Farm Workers Association (NFWA). Their goals included better housing, increased wages, clean drinking water and field toilets. They also endeavored to register farm workers to vote. When the union's flag was unveiled, there was a mixed reaction, even shock. The black eagle set against a red background seemed too strong, even similar to a communist symbol. But the design was approved, and the block design shape of the eagle was easy to recognize and simple to copy.

In 1965 Chávez led 2000 NFWA members on a strike demanding better wages for grape pickers in Delano, California. The growers were a small but powerful group, so Chávez had to use unusual tactics to get the attention and support of the public. He led a 340-mile march from Delano to Sacramento that brought national attention to the strike. Workers and supporters carried banners with the black eagle emblem, the chosen union symbol, and the slogan, VIVA LA CAUSA! ("Long live the cause"). In addition to the march, Chávez went on a water-only fast for 25 days to emphasize the nonviolent philosophy of his cause. The following year the NFWA and the grape pickers' union merged to create the United Farm Workers with Chávez as president.

In 1968 Chávez took the national spotlight by calling for all consumers nationwide to stop buying grapes grown in California. His timing coincided with the existence of sympathetic anti-war, anti-government protest groups across the country, and many people rallied to action, including boycotting grapes. This boycott was highly successful as many churches, student groups and political organizations backed the effort. By 1970 many growers were forced to sign union contracts that established basic facilities and rights for the workers. A law was passed that gave farm workers the right to join unions without being fired.

Chávez continued to lead more boycotts, especially against the use of pesticides, but he never experienced the same success again. With the grape boycott, the right combination of obvious worker hardship, public sentiment and strong leadership by Chávez all came together, galvanizing the country to demand for a change that could not be ignored.

César Chávez died peacefully in his sleep on April 23, 1993, in the small village of San Luis near Yuma, Arizona, where he was born. More than 40,000 people participated in his funeral. The following year President Clinton posthumously awarded Chávez the nation's highest civilian award, the Presidential Medal of Freedom. California now celebrates March 31, Chávez's birthday, as an official state holiday.

WANGARI MAATHAI
(1940–2011)

Significance: For her work with the Green Belt Movement in East Africa, in 2004 Maathai was the first African woman and first environmentalist to win the Nobel Peace Prize.

Wangari Muta was born April 1, 1940, in Nyeri, Kenya, when the country was still a British colony. Nyeri is northeast of Nairobi in the fertile rolling hill country of the Central Highlands where coffee and tea were planted by white settlers in the late 19th and early 20th centuries. She was the third child of Muta Wanjuga and Lydia Wanjiru Muta. As a young girl Wangari was average in size and physical coordination, and her strongest features were her flashing smile, laughing eyes and quick intelligence. At the suggestion of her eldest brother, Nderitu, her parents, farmers belonging to the major Kenyan Kikuyu tribe, sent her to a boarding school where she could get a good education. Boarding school education is common in many African countries, but the institutions are generally very spartan with the barest of amenities. During the 1940s in Kenya, it was unusual for a girl to attend school, particularly beyond an early elementary level. Because Muta excelled, her teachers in secondary school helped her gain a scholarship to a college in Kansas, where she earned a degree in biology, followed by a master's degree in biology from the University of Pittsburgh in Pennsylvania in 1966. In Kansas she was known as Mary Jo.

Muta was in the United States for five years during the height of the equal rights struggle for African Americans, and she was deeply influenced by the demonstration of the power of democracy. She has since remarked: "I can sincerely say that my coming to America was a great opening of the eyes for me. It gave me a completely different horizon, a different perception, and it gave me some values that I have tried to share, and it really made me who I am."

Muta continued doctoral studies in Germany and at the University of Nairobi, where she was awarded a PhD in 1971 in veterinary anatomy. She began teaching at the university and became chair of the department. Muta was the first woman to earn a PhD and to attain such a position in East and Central Africa. Her commitment to her home country is noteworthy; very many Africans who study abroad for years and earn advanced degrees choose not to return to work in their home country, a condition known as "brain drain."

In 1969 Muta married businessman and aspiring politician Mwangi Maathai. In 1974 her husband decided to seek a seat in Kenya's parliament, and as she campaigned at his side, her awareness of concerns of the people grew, especially the issue of no jobs. She saw that most conflict was caused by competition for resources of water and land.

In addition to her university teaching, Maathai became involved with women's affairs, and in 1976 she introduced the idea of planting trees as a means of conserving the environment. She noticed how much effort rural women must expend to search for and cut firewood to fuel their cookers, and she saw the disastrous long term consequences of deforestation. The Greenbelt Movement was born, which has resulted in the planting of millions of trees on farms, schools, church properties and public lands. The Greenbelt Movement has subsequently spread to other African countries where similar tree planting initiatives are developing.

The nickname of Tree Lady is often used for Maathai. Wangari and Mwangi Maathai had three children: Waweru, Wanjira and Muta. Wanjira Mathai (she uses a different spelling) was a close aide to her mother in the Greenbelt Movement.

Maathai led protests against land grabbing schemes and illegal logging, activities that landed her in jail more than once. In the course of her activism she was the subject of beatings by police. Once while she was replanting a forest illegally cut down by developers, guards beat her; she signed the police report in her own blood. She was once denounced by President Daniel arap Moi as a "mad woman." She had to spend time in hiding and move around Kenya in disguises. Some of her colleagues disappeared or were killed.

The Greenbelt Movement seeks not only to plant trees in designated areas but also to prevent the destruction of Kenya's forests. From different directions there are various threats to the country's forests. Wealthy business interests engage in unrestricted logging or clear-cutting for timber and development. When the indigenous trees are cut, tree farmers plant quick-growing non-natives that will be harvested for income in a relatively short time. Desperate people raid the forests for firewood and building materials, and sometimes small plots are cleared illegally for growing crops. The government typically looks the other direction, either due to incompetence or even bribery.

When the authoritarian government of Moi supported the construction of a 62-story office tower building on the grounds of Uruhu Park, Maathai led a successful protest to keep the open-space in downtown Nairobi free for family-style gatherings and public rallies. Moi was furious and said that the development's opponents, many of them women, had "insects in their heads." Maathai's group prevailed, but the Greenbelt members were denounced as "ill-informed divorcees." Later, in 2006, then U.S. Senator Barack Obama traveled to Kenya. She and the Senator met and planted a tree together in Uhuru Park.

Gender continued to be an issue. In 1980 her husband filed for divorce, famously declaring that Maathai was "too educated, too strong, too successful, too stubborn and too hard to control." In an interview with *The New York Times* in 1989, referring to the Uhuru Park incident and responding to the attitude toward women, she is quoted as saying: "They can't stand a woman who stands up. I'm being seen as an arrogant woman because I dare to object. I call them arrogant."

Many of the poorest countries in Africa borrow large sums of money from rich, lender nations, and in reality there is no possibility of repayment in the foreseeable future. Maathai campaigned for such foreign debts to be canceled among developing countries in order that their economies have a fighting chance of healthy growth.

In the late 1980s Maathai founded the Green Party in Kenya and ran for president without success. In 2002 she was elected to Kenya's parliament (one of 18 women for a 222-member body) and was appointed assistant minister for the environment. She lost a bid for reelection in December 2007, primarily because she refused to compromise and bow to tribal politics. She held high hopes for democracy in Kenya, but she also expressed the need for patience, for as she saw it, the transition to democracy is a slow process.

There was some international criticism when she was awarded the Nobel Peace Prize in 2004 because her work has not involved bringing peace between conflicting nations. The Nobel's committee chose her because they see the peace that results when people are not fighting over water, food and other natural resources; the Greenbelt Movement plants seeds of peace by working toward sustainable development of resources.

Wangari Maathai traveled extensively and was active as a speaker for environmental causes. In person she radiated warmth and energy, laughing and gesturing with enthusiasm for her audiences and speaking in a lilting East African accent. She was a strong woman who had faced conflict bravely.

In African lore there are many references to the three-legged stool, and Maathai used the image to explain her work. According to her, the three legs represent the environment, democracy and peace. Lacking any of the three, the stool cannot stand. The seat of the stool represents the future development for the country, because the successful future depends upon the three legs being secure enough for the citizens to work creatively for solutions.

Wangari Maathai died on September 25, 2011, from complications while receiving treatment for cancer at a Nairobi hospital. In 2012, Wangari Gardens opened in Washington, D.C.; it is a community garden project that honors the legacy of Maathai and her mission for community engagement and environmental protection.

BIBLIOGRAPHY

Adams, Jerome R. *Latin American Heroes*, New York: Random House, 1991.

Alter, Judith. *Eli Whitney*, New York: Franklin Watts, 1990.

Anderson, Mary Anne, Stephanie M. Hamilton and Karen Martin Tryda. *International Biographies*, Rocky River, Ohio: The Center for Learning, 1992.

Basel, Roberta. *Sequoyah, Inventor of Written Cherokee*, Minneapolis, MN: Compass Point Books, 2007.

Borden, Louise. *Sea Clocks,* New York: Simon and Schuster, 2004.

Collier, James Lincoln. *The Clara Barton You Never Knew,* New York: Children's Press, 2003.

Collins, Gail. *America's Women*, New York: William Morrow, 2003.

Conner, Edwina. *Marie Curie*, New York: Bookwright Press, 1987.

Cooke, Alastair. *America*, New York: Alfred A. Knopf, Inc., 1973.

Cooper, Floyd. *Mandela*, New York: Philomel Books, 1996.

Cottingham, Jan. "Wangari Maathai," WorldArk, Heifer International, Nov./Dec. 2005

Dash, Joan. *The Longitude Prize*, New York: Farrar, Straus and Giroux, 2000.

De Varona, Frank. *Simón Bolivar*, New York: Houghton Mifflin, 1993.

Demi. *Gandhi*, New York: Margaret K. McElderry Books, 2001.

Feinstein, Stephen. *César Chávez*, Berkeley Heights, NJ: Enslow Publishers, 2004.

Foster, Leila Merrell. *Nien Cheng, Courage in China*, Chicago: Children's Press, 1992.

Hakim, Joy. *A History of Us,* New York: Oxford University Press, 1999.

Hasday, Judy L. *Marie Curie, Pioneer on the Frontier of Radioactivity*, Berkeley Heights, NJ: Enslow Publishers, Inc. 2004.

Kabaji, Egara. *Jomo Kenyatta, Father of Harambee, Nairobi*, Kenya: Sasa Sema Publ. Ltd., 2000.

Keller, Helen. *The Story of My Life*, New York: Penguin Books, 1988.

Klausner, Janet. *Sequoyah's Gift*, New York: HarperCollins Publishers, 1993.

Kolpas, Norman. *Mao*, London: Cameron and Taylor Ltd., 1981.

Kramer, Ann. *Mandela*, Washington, D.C.: National Geographic, 2005.

Lifton, Betty Jean. *The King of Children*, New York: Farrar, Straus and Giroux, 1988.

Madarshahi, Mehri. *About Wangari Maathai*, unesco. org, March 2005.

Malaspina, Ann. *The Chinese Revolution and Mao Zedong in World History,* Berkeley Heights, NJ: Enslow Publishers, 2004.

Mandela, Nelson. "The Sacred Warrior," *Time Magazine*, January 3, 2000.

McKissack, Patricia and Fredrick. *Frederick Douglass: Leader Against Slavery*, Berkeley Heights, NJ: Enslow Publishers, Inc., 2002.

Menzies, Gavin. *1421*, New York: HarperCollins Publishers Inc., 2003.

Meredith, Martin. "Brand Mandela, Controlling a Legend," *Christian Science Monitor,* March 12, 2008.

Petry, Ann. *Harriet Tubman, Conductor on the Underground Railroad*, New York: Crowell, 1955.

Severance, John B. *Gandhi, Great Soul*, New York: Clarion Books, 1997.

Skelton, Renee. *Harriet Tubman, A Woman of Courage*, New York: HarperCollins, 2005.

Sobel, Dava. *Longitude,* London: Penguin Books Ltd, 1996.

Soto, Gary. *César Chávez, A Hero for Everyone*, New York: Aladdin Paperbacks, 2003.

Spence, Jonathan D. "Mao Zedong," *Time Magazine*, April 13, 1998.

Staley, Betty. *Hear the Voice of the Griot*, Fair Oaks, CA: Rudolf Steiner College Press, 1998.

Stewart, Whitney. *Mao Zedong*, Minneapolis: Twenty-First Century Books, 2006.

Syme, Ronald. *Bolivar, The Liberator*, New York: William and Morrow, 1967.

Wepman, Dennis. *Helen Keller Humanitarian*, New York: Chelsea House, 1987.

Wilson, Mitchell. *American Science and Invention: A Pictorial History*, New York: Simon and Schuster, 1954.

BIOGRAPHY REPORTS

The list of names below is provided for choosing or assigning for individual student reports.

Addams, Jane—reformer
Anthony, Susan B.—feminist
Armstrong, Neil—astronaut, U.S. Senator
Banneker, Richard—scientist
Bell, Alexander Graham—inventor
Boone, Daniel—explorer
Brown, John—anti-slavery activist
Carnegie, Andrew—industrialist
Carver, George Washington—scientist
Castro, Fidel—Cuban leader
Cather, Willa—author
Chiang Kai-shek—Chinese leader
Chief Joseph—Nez Perce tribe leader
Churchill, Winston—British prime minister
Copland, Aaron—American musician
Darwin, Charles—scientist, evolutionist
Du Bois, W.E.B.—African-American leader
Earhart, Amelia—aviator
Edison, Thomas—inventor
Einstein, Albert—scientist, professor
Emerson, Ralph Waldo—poet, writer

Ford, Henry—automobile maker, creator of assembly line

Freidan, Betty—feminist

Fulton, Robert—steam engine inventor

Gershwin, George—American musician

Goldman, Emma—anti-war activist

Gorbachev, Mikhail—Soviet leader

Hitler, Adolph—Third Reich despotic leader

Jackson, Andrew "Stonewall"—17th U.S. President

Lenin, Vladimir—creator of Communist Party in Russia

Lewis, Merriweather and William Clark—explorers

Lindberg, Charles—navigator, pilot

Marshall, Thurgood—Supreme Court justice

Marx, Karl—formulator of socialism

McCormick, Cyrus—inventor of the reaper

Monet, Claude—impressionist painter

Morse, Samuel—inventor of the telegraph

Mother Theresa—religious leader, activist

Muir, John—naturalist

Nation, Carry—temperance movement activist

Nicholas II—Russian czar

Parks, Rosa—civil rights activist

Picasso, Pablo—artist

Powell, Adam Clayton—U.S. Senator

Queen Elizabeth II—modern Queen of England

Queen Liliuokalani—Hawaiian monarch

Queen Victoria—British monarch

Remarque, Erich Marie—anti-war author

Rhodes, Cecil—leader of British empire in Africa

Rivera, Diego—Mexican artist
Rockefeller, John D.—industrialist, philanthropist
Roosevelt, Franklin—32nd President
Roosevelt, Theodore—27th President
Sacajawea—guide to Lewis and Clark
Schweitzer, Albert—doctor, humanitarian
Stanley, Henry and David Livingstone—explorers in
    Africa
Stowe, Harriet Beecher—anti-slavery activist
Thoreau, Henry David—writer, philosopher
Truth, Sojourner—anti-slavery activist
Tutu, Desmond—South Africa leader
Twain, Mark (Samuel Clemens)—author
Villa, Pancho—Mexican revolutionary
Washington, Booker T.—educator
Watt, James—steam engine inventor
Whitman, Walt—poet
Wright, Orville and Wilbur—builders of the first
    successful airplane

Made in the USA
Middletown, DE
09 January 2021

30520548R00084